# EMBRYO FACTORY

## FACTORY

### THE STEM CELL WARS

A NOVEL

# EMBRYO FACTORY

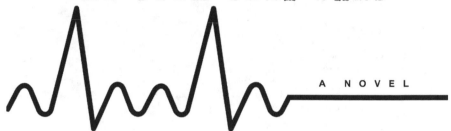

THE STEM CELL WARS

A NOVEL

## REV. RICHARD A. HUMPHREY
## DR. LOREN J. HUMPHREY

PRESS

ACW Press
Eugene, Oregon 97405

**Embryo Factory: The Stem Cell Wars**
Copyright ©2003 Richard A. Humphrey and Loren J. Humphrey
All rights reserved

Cover Design by Alpha Advertising
Interior design by Pine Hill Graphics

Packaged by ACW Press
5501 N. 7th Ave., #502
Phoenix, Arizona 85013
www.acwpress.com
The views expressed or implied in this work do not necessarily reflect those of ACW Press. Ultimate design, content, and editorial accuracy of this work is the responsibility of the author(s).

Library of Congress Cataloging-in-Publication Data
*(Provided by Quality Books Inc.)*

Humphrey, Richard A., 1936-
 Embryo factory : the stem cell wars / by Richard A.
 Humphrey, Loren J. Humphrey ; introduction by Rollin A.
 Van Broekhoven
  p. cm.
  ISBN 1-932124-08-X

  1. Stem cells--Research--Moral and ethical aspects--
Fiction. 2. Human cloning--Research--Moral and ethical
aspects--Fiction. 3. Appalachian Region--Fiction.
I. Humphrey, Loren, 1931-  II. Title.

PS3608.U568E63 2003          813'.6
                             QBI33-1190

**Printed in the United States of America.**

## Acknowledgments

The idea for this novel arose from a symposium sponsored by the Oxford Society of Scholars, Dayton, Tennessee. Viewpoints expressed in the debate that followed the presentation of papers by the authors and the Hon. Rollin Van Broekhoven form some of the dialogue in this work. We are grateful for the points made by the members of the Society and faculty members of Oxford Graduate School, Dayton, Tennessee.

The authors wish to thank Dr. Van Broekhoven for his encouragement, ideas, and crisp, meaningful introduction to the novel. As a Christian active on the faculty of the Oxford Graduate School and a federal judge on the Board of Contract Appeals in Washington, D.C. he is uniquely qualified to prepare the reader for the moral, ethical, and legal issues portrayed in this work.

Special thanks go to Donald Brenner, Professor Emeritus, the University of Missouri School of Journalism for his diligence and expertise in editing the manuscript.

# Introduction

In 1729, during a period when the Irish were crushed by poverty and the brutal economic policies of the British overlords, Jonathan Swift, a conservative Irish pastor and satirist, wrote his book, A Modest Proposal. In this book, he suggested that Irish babies could be sold for food. That way there would be both more food to go around and fewer mouths to feed. Besides, baby skin would make soft leather. This would improve the Irish economy by creating a new industry that would create jobs. Swift was lampooning the utilitarianism of the Enlightenment, which taught that anything could be morally justified if it were "useful" giving the greatest tangible benefit to the greatest number. Swift's A Modest Proposal did wake the conscience of many of his readers, who realized that no social end could ever justify the consumption of babies and that no moral philosophy that could propose such an end could be valid.

Thinking in such utilitarian philosophical terms has, however, become ingrained in the way Americans think about many social issues, including in-vitro fertilization, genetic engineering, stem cell research, and cloning, for example. If something, like embryonic stem cell research can produce wonderful results in curing many debilitating diseases, then, how could such a practice be bad? These are the issues addressed by the authors in this book.

If the latter half of the twentieth century is regarded as the Information Age, the beginning of the twenty-first century may be considered the Biotechnology Age. Advances made in scientific research frequently, if not always, are made before a consensus on the moral, political, and legal issues surrounding the particular scientific research has been reached. Fundamental disagreements about these matters make the debates seem interminable.

Debates regarding biotechnology in the 1990s and extending to early 2001 were largely confined to whether the United States government should fund stem cell research and cloning. Except with respect to cloning, these debates did not address the issues of whether stem cell research and cloning should be morally permissible or whether the research should be legally permitted or proscribed through legislation or court decision.

According to a report issued by the National Institutes of Health, and much of the lay literature concerning stem cell research, stem cells hold the key to replacing cells lost in many diseases. The report states that there is little doubt that this potential benefit underpins the vast interest about stem cell research. Some of the diseases identified in the report include Parkinson's disease, diabetes, chronic heart disease, end-stage kidney disease, liver failure, and cancer. In addition, stem cells may be used to generate replacement tissues for treating neurological diseases, such as spinal cord injury, multiple sclerosis, and Alzheimer's disease. Neither significant scientific proof that this was the case, nor that damage or horrible aberrations of human existence could occur, assuaged those determined to continue to advance the course of science with government funding. Possible moral claims against such research and biotechnological practices exerted little influence.

A stem cell is a special kind of cell that has a unique capacity to renew itself and to give rise to specialized cell types. Most cells in the body are committed to conduct a specific function, although stem cells are found in differentiated or specialized tissue in the adult. Stem cells are uncommitted and remain uncommitted until they receive a signal to develop into specialized cells. The proliferative capacity of stem cells, combined with the ability to become specialized, makes them unique.

Through animal research, scientists discovered a class of cells that could develop into any cell type in the body. These cells were called "pluripotent," which means that these cells have the potential to develop into all of the more than two hundred different known cell forms. In 1998, scientists for the first time were able to isolate this class of pluripotent stem cell from early human embryos and grow them in a culture. This discovery spawned the controversy and reignited the basis of the abortion feud of previous decades, "When is an embryo or fetus a being?" By utilizing fictional characters, this novel thrusts the consequences of moral bankruptcy into everyday life and plunges the reader into the maelstrom of deep-seated emotions.

Christian philosopher, apologist, and debater Ravi Zacharias wrote many years ago that ideas that shape and inform culture and people are passed down in one of three ways. At the basic foundational or theoretical level or substructure, ideas and belief systems are communicated from generation to generation through the use of the writings of great thinkers, such as Plato, Socrates, Aristotle, Augustine, Aquinas, Calvin, or some of the Enlightenment thinkers, such as Hume or Kant, for example. These are the basic ideas of reality, morals, and values that come from the intellectual, philosophical, and academic communities that inform how people see and identify themselves and their culture.

At a secondary level, culture may be influenced aesthetically, that is, by an invasion of the imagination by the arts. Few people read the ancient and classical writings of Plato, Socrates, and Aristotle, the Enlightenment thinkers, or even those of a postmodernist bent in academia. Therefore, the popular media and entertainment sectors of our society usually inform our contact with the world of ideas. In other words, what is portrayed in entertainment sectors and media outlets of our society reinforces ideas of reality, morality, and values. Although informed by the theoretical level, this secondary level forms the infrastructure through which belief systems are passed down from generation to generation and inform and shape the culture.

The third level is what Ravi Zacharias calls the prescriptive and superstructure level. At this level, we receive our ideas of reality, morality, and values, from family and friends around "the kitchen table." Frequently these ideas are based on traditional religious beliefs passed down through the church and through generations of families and communities. These ideas and beliefs may also be informed by the popular talk show hosts and guests on radio and television, where experts and guests talk about everything from environment and global warming, from health to psychology, from abortion to gay rights, and from human rights to animal rights with equal authority. However, too frequently these ideas and beliefs, when presented outside the safe environment of the home, lose their plausibility when contrasted with what has been presented in the popular media.

Most people, including many who are well-read, have not seriously thought about the bioethical issues presented in this book. They have gained some insights from the popular media of theater, movies, television, music, and the press, which stress the potential promise of some of the biotechnological research, without regard to the moral or public policy consideration, and whether, indeed, the promise of these cures and advances is even scientifically achievable.

This is the point where the authors of this book address these questions, portraying lifelike settings that present drama brought about by competing ideas of scientific advancement, and competing and contrasting concepts of reality and morality. Much of the development of this subject in dramatic form undoubtedly came from the papers and discussions held at a symposium on science, bioethics, and law or public policy held at a forum of the Oxford Society of Scholars. Although these papers were presented in theoretical and scholarly format, and the discussions that followed were on an academic level, this book presents a real-life drama of the interwoven influences of science, ethical theory and moral reasoning, religious commitment, and public policy as expressed through the medium of law. This is a book that invades the imagination and aesthetic with complicated relationships and complex moral issues. Perhaps it will spur thought in these important areas of modern culture that will go beyond the mere prescriptive form frequently found in third prescriptive and superstructure level identified above.

To update the "modest proposal" made by Jonathan Swift, "we are facing a similar modest proposal, but it is dead serious." Namely,

> Since the original cells of a fetus can develop into all the organs of a human body, why not use these so-called "stem cells" to regenerate damaged tissue in adults? Doctors could grind up all that fetal tissue from abortions and unwanted test-tube embryos at the fertility clinics into really good medicine.
>
> Harvesting embryonic children for their stem cells is little different from Swift's proposal to harvest just-born children for food. But whereas Swift's audience pulled back in revulsion, much of the American public thinks this is a swell idea.

Rollin A. Van Broekhoven, JD, LLM, DPhil, DLitt, DPS
Washington, D.C.

# Prologue

"**No.** Not yet." The lanky man pushed aside the bushes in front of him and stared at a gray structure twenty yards away, the rear of the chapel. He grabbed an arm of his companion, who rocked from knee to knee. Moving close to the pockmarked face he lowered his voice and said, "Get yer thumb off the button. I'm goin' round to the side. See?" He pointed with a gnarled finger. "There's light shinin' on the ground from the kitchen. I'll take a look over there. We'd better make certain that preacher's not in the kitchen. We ain't supposed to kill him—just scare him. Ezrah, hunker down and hush up." He eased through the bushes and dashed into the shadows of the building.

Ezrah watched the figure disappear in the shadows. Bright light from an auto turning onto Highway 421 momentarily lit up the parking lot to his left. He removed the weather-beaten straw hat, took a rag from a rear pocket and wiped the sweat from his forehead, but kept his beady eyes fixed toward the side of the house. A breeze picked up, moving the ancient, tall trees that guarded the small chapel and the parsonage thirty yards to the right, their movement making the moonlight dance on the grass and casting eerie ghost-like figures on the illuminated side of the house. The gray figure of his companion burst through the bushes and kneeled next to him, his chest heaving to catch his breath.

Ezrah raised off his haunches onto his knees. "Seed him, Mort?" He let a vacillating stream of air sound a chuckle while he replaced his hat and stuffed the rag in a rear pocket.

"Didn't see preacher." Mort made a soft giggle. "But I sawed a womer get a beer from the frig. Nobody in the kitchen now. Wait 'til they find that womer with the preacher—and them drinkin' beer. Won't think he's so high and mighty then." He turned and searched Ezrah's eyes. He took the hand with the black object. "Ready to blow a hole in 'er? You'll be five hundred jack richer and all our 'ens' folks will keep their jobs at the factory, Ezrah." He pulled the jumpy man to his feet. "Come on. Let's get 'er done." He pushed through the bushes, glancing over his shoulder as Ezrah followed to the chapel. On the far side he pulled Ezrah behind the cinder-block structure.

Ezrah clutched the black object, raised it to his face and hovered an index finger over the red button. "Can I blow 'er?" His eyes danced, black beads in the pale moonlight.

"You 'en can watch. Just look round the corner so's you can see, but not far so's you 'en don't get hit by nothin'." Mort stood and stooped as he peered around the chapel corner above Ezrah. "Blow 'er."

A deafening explosion sent a rush of wind that peppered the chapel and blew off Ezrah's hat. Mort pulled Ezrah back, his eyes big as an owl's. "What the—that bomb was so small, it couldn't have blowed a shanty over. Whoo-ee. What happened?" Both men peeked around the corner and watched flames engulf the house, the side closest to them gone. Flames shot above treetops, lighting the sky. "Let's git. We 'ens gotta clear outa here."

They ran across the parking lot, through a stand of birch, jumped a small gully and came to a pickup parked on a narrow gravel road just off of Route 421. A floppy-eared hound, tied in the back of the truck, whined. "Shush, dog," Mort said, and climbed behind the wheel. He turned to Ezrah, fidgeting in the passenger seat. "We 'ens gettin' way up this here mountain and do some coon huntin'. When they ask us, we 'ens hunted from dark to near dawn."

"What about this 'un?" Ezrah waved the black box.

Mort snatched it and stuffed it in a shirt pocket. "I'll smash it and bury it up there." He threw a hand toward Pine Mountain and started the motor.

"Mort?"

"Yeah."

"I ain't feelin so good. Preacher sure 'nuf stirred up trouble, takin' money outa mouths—our sister got hundreds of jack fir giving eggs—but some womer was with the preacher. She warn't doin' no harm. And he didn't do 'nuthin bad 'nuf to die fer."

"Preacher done called this business of getting a womer's—they're called ovums, not eggs..." He paused as he maneuvered the rickety truck onto a narrow side road and through a shallow wash. "They make 'em fertile from a man's juice and then study them. Important for helping fight diseases. But preacher says it's a sin and he even said he was declaring war on those doin' such a bad thing." Mort stole a quick glance at Ezrah. "Lotsa innocent folk gets killed in a war, Ezrah."

The forty-year-old pickup rattled and strained up the winding mountain road. Mort whistled, but stopped momentarily to let Ezrah open the door and empty his stomach contents on the gravel. At a switchback the road hugged the mountain edge, offering a clear view of the sky and the valley below. Directly below, the sky was bright orange, the fire from the burning parsonage painting the nearby chapel spire a dancing silver-yellow, even casting enough light to reveal ghostly outlines of some buildings in Baxter.

Mort stopped the truck, scooted over and leaned in front of Ezrah to peer out the door window. He studied his nervous brother. "Feelin' poorly? Look sorta pale."

Ezrah made a smile, his jagged teeth looking sinister in the pale moonlight. "I'm alright. Wow! Looks like a gully burner from here. And looky. A bunch of ants runnin' round the fire, as if they was a doin' a dance."

Mort moved back behind the wheel, reached under the seat and thrust a paper bag in front of Ezrah. "Take this poke. This here 'shine will settle yer stomach. We 'ens best get to coon huntin'."

Ezrah gulped a mouthful of moonshine and stared at the bottle shining from the moonlight that penetrated the torn spot in the bag. "Ma wouldn't cotton to us killin' nobody, specially a preacher. If'n Pa were livin' he sure would wop us 'ens good."

"Ha. Pa probably would have hepped us. And fer the blast bein' bigger than we planned, he'd say God meant it so."

"How you figgerin' that, Mort?" Ezrah emptied the poke and chucked it out the window.

"He'd say it weren't no accident we decided to put that there poke bomb where it'd make such a big blast. Must've blown up a gas stove. Mighty fine blast—weren't it?"

Mort pulled the truck into a clearing, turned off the lights and climbed out. He untied the floppy-eared hound and looked at Ezrah across the truck bed. "Hush up. Don't pay no mind. Act like nuthin' happened. We 'ens don't know nuthin' 'cause we been huntin' all night." He helped the hound jump to the ground, and pulled back on the leash as the anxious beast strained to start the hunt, raising its brown-spotted head, sniffing the air and then the ground. The moon escaped from behind a cloud and painted the wavy grass of the meadow a silver-blue.

Mort started as the hound dragged him along the edge of the meadow. "A great night fer coon huntin', Ezrah. Ain't it great to be free, to be alive?"

Ezrah didn't answer. He had dashed back to the truck to get his old straw hat.

Chapter

# ONE

"I will stop them from killing embryos," Pastor Milton Heiter said, and wrinkled the end of his long narrow nose when he recognized the disinfectant odor of hospital sheets. From under the covers, he glanced around the room, recognized the décor of Appalachia Regional Hospital, in Harlan, Kentucky. He froze his gaze, a defiant look, on the burly figure leaning over the foot of the bed. The man's eyes, their steel-gray outlined by a thin black line, mocked the reverend.

"You may not live long enough to get a chance," said the leaning man. "We've been over that for the past half hour." He removed a pad from his inside coat pocket. "Come on, Milt…"

"Milton to you, Inspector, whatever your name is," the pastor said. "And write fast because I'll only tell you once more. It was about ten and I turned off the lights in my quarters. Have you seen it?"

The inspector asked, "The wreck of a trailer behind the parsonage—thirty feet from where the parsonage sat before a blast demolished it? You really call that your quarters?"

"Two days ago that gully-washer flooded Abe and his wife out of their cabin, so I moved them..." Milton Heiter blinked back tears, stared at the off-white ceiling and continued. "So they were the ones—the bodies you found in the ruins. Good folk. Why did the tanks have to blow?" He scrunched up his face. "Why? I haven't had them turned on since March. Didn't use the heater, and the stove is electric."

"Reverend, I told you before—that concussion got your memory—I told you we found evidence at the site that a bomb blew the tanks, and I doubt it was meant for them. It was meant for you." FBI Agent Maxwell Tooms narrowed his eyes, searching Heiter's face, a map of a day's growth mingled with dried bloody dots. Tooms held onto the lapels of his light blue suit. The white cotton shirt was open at the top, the dark blue tie hanging loosely. The man's receding hairline gave him a prominent forehead. Gray-speckled black hair, partially covering his ears, seemed unruly.

Heiter squeezed his eyelids together, exhaled a rush of air. With cracked, dry lips barely parted he said, "Now I have a personal reason to stop them from killing embryos, Detective Tums."

"It's Agent Tooms. We'll find who set off the bomb, and they'll lead us to the person who wants you out of the way, Milton." He stood, his protuberant belly trying to pop the button of his coat. He closed the pad. A young woman in a long white coat entered. He turned, nodded, and stopped in the doorway. "I called for my associate to come from Washington. When you leave the hospital, I'll have some protection for you."

"How is it you showed up so fast? You stationed in Washington?" Milton asked while gently exploring his face, rubbing the brown stubble and pausing over the larger of the numerous dark red dots.

"I was ordered to come down and investigate—see who stirs up trouble. Been here two weeks," Tooms said.

"Then you know I'm not the troublemaker," Heiter said.

"How am I supposed to know that?"

"If you've been here two weeks you should have learned that I'm a pacifist, non-violence. The demonstrations I lead are peaceful. You…"

Tooms waved the notepad at Heiter. "Concussion sure 'nuf has gotten your memory. The march two weeks ago erupted into violence. From what I hear, it was as about as bad as when Harlan Home Guard took on the Confederate Virginians in Cumberland Gap during the Civil War. According to John Fox Jr. this area always has been prone to violence. There's been a lot of bushwhacking, killing, and family feuds in these mountains. That's why I was sent here, that and to check out Curewell Clinic."

"When the violence erupted, I called off the march and all but the outsiders, the troublemakers, went back to the church with me," Heiter said.

Tooms smirked. "You don't believe in killing. I suppose you disapproved of the war and killing of Islamic terrorists after they flew our planes into the World Trade Center in New York? Their Koran told them to kill us infidels."

"Islamic radicals, wild dogs, Tooms," Heiter said.

The woman stepped toward the bed and spoke, "Reverend, Jesus said almost the same. 'I came not to send peace, but a sword.'"

Heiter bristled. "I heard that. Some atheist from Wisconsin tried to say the Bible is no better than the Koran. Note, Jesus said He came to send a sword. He didn't say, 'Here's a sword. Go kill Islamic people.' What he meant was that when Christians follow His teachings, others will kill them. How true. The sword and lions killed the early Christians, and Islam's radicals slaughtered Christ's followers during the Middle Ages."

The woman seemed to buy the explanation and said, "Agent Tooms asked what a pacifist, a believer in non-violence, thought about us killing the terrorists."

The woman was irritating. Heiter frowned, shrugged and said, "Every now and then one has to kill a mad dog. We had to kill

Hitler, a mad dog, or else he would have killed six million more Jews. I don't like it, but sometimes it must be. God understands."

Tooms turned to the woman. "Doctor, when will the reverend be discharged?"

"Maybe two days," she said as she approached the foot of the bed.

Happy for the change in topic, Milton Heiter said, "You look too young to be a doctor." He raised on an elbow, grimaced, and collapsed back on the bed.

The dark-haired woman pulled her white coat together and leaned over the foot of the bed. "Name's Doctor Benz, Susan Benz." She scrutinized the bruised face. "I just finished internship at UK in Lexington, so I'm young, twenty-six. But I'm a doctor, a good one—on the staff at Daniel Boone Clinic right next door."

"I'm out of here today. My parishioners need me to appear, to show them I'm okay—and to help them grieve the loss of two fine brethren."

"You have a mild concussion. Can't even sit, so..." Before she could finish, Heiter shoved to a sitting position, uttering a faint moan. Benz moved around to the side of the bed and grabbed an arm.

"If you don't sign me out, I'll leave anyway." He stared past her to the doorway. "And if the FBI are going to baby-sit me, I'll teach them about the Lord. From what I've seen they could use a lot of religion."

"Your behavior fits the description portrayed by the Lexington Herald. You don't have any clothes and nowhere to go," Benz said.

Tooms cleared his throat. "You got the concussion when the blast threw you against that trailer you call quarters. Not much left to sleep a person."

"I'll sleep in the office at the back of the church. It has a bathroom. That's where I was headed when the house blew."

"What you say, doc? I need to know so I can arrange his protection."

Benz removed a penlight from a coat pocket, sat on the edge of the bed, and shined it in one eye and then the other. She replaced the light and held Heiter's chin. She turned his head toward her and stuck a finger before his eyes. "Follow my finger."

Obediently, Heiter's eyes followed the finger from left to right, right to left, then up and down.

From the doorway, Tooms said, "That eye looks awful. Will his vision be okay?"

Benz looked over her shoulder and said, "Subconjunctival hemorrhage from the blast. Looks worse than it is. He can go in two days if no complications appear."

"Like what, Doctor Benz?" Heiter asked, his face covered with a frown.

Benz rubbed a finger lightly down his nose. "Cracked nose— that gave you the black eye and the blast caused the red-black eyeball." She grabbed a hand and aimed it behind his head. "Feel. Several stitches closed a gash."

Heiter winced when he felt the back of his head. "And my sore chest?"

"Two cracked ribs. Chest Xray in emergency showed possible damage to the lung. That's the big reason—and the concussion— why we need to observe you in the hospital a couple days."

Heiter eased back on the pillow and closed his eyes tightly. Tears gathered in the corners of his eyes, slowly streamed over high cheekbones. "Doctor, on your way out would you ask the nurse to bring me a Bible?" He dried his eyes with the sleeve of the gown and watched as Benz motioned Tooms to leave. She leaned close, her blue-green eyes warm and locked on his watery ones. "Reverend Heiter, I am your doctor. I tend your physical ailments and, along with them, your inner wounds."

Heiter liked the way the end of her turned-up nose wiggled when she talked. Generous lips of her small round mouth had only a suggestion of lipstick. "Thanks." He closed his eyes again.

At the door Benz stepped back and said, "I'll get you a Bible. Please take the pill a nurse will bring. See you this evening. I always see patients before I leave for home. Try to rest."

Milton Heiter heard her footsteps fade. He opened his eyes and stared, searching the false ceiling of his room. "Lord, my physical aches pale in the presence of the pain I feel for the Caulders. I meant for them to have shelter, not burn to death. Please…" Footsteps interrupted his plea.

A graying, somewhat plump nurse with a cherub smile swept into the room. At the sink she filled a glass and put an angled straw in it. Peering through the upper portion of her bifocals she said, "Reverend, take this pill. You need some rest. It'll get you out of here for Sunday's service."

Heiter took the small pink pill, put it on his tongue and put his lips around the straw. After taking in a mouthful he swallowed, at the same time reading the nurse's name tag. He leaned back and forced a faint smile. "Thanks, Mrs. Rawlins. That woman doctor seems young but pretty good at her business."

"She is a very good doctor, but could use your help with her personal life, like you did for my Jenny, Pastor."

Heiter searched his memory bank, but failed to pull up any recollection of her Jenny. He smiled. "Well, I guess if Doctor Benz gets me well, I can see what I can do for her problems." He watched the nurse smile and depart, the scene seeming to fade into gray, fuzzy clouds.

The trip to radiology and the exertion to stand before the machine had sapped Heiter of his usual late afternoon surge of energy. The evening meal arrived and he nibbled, more out of habit than hunger. Staring out the window he looked across the street at the Cumberland Valley Technical School and the National Guard Armory in the distance. He smiled when his gaze ran over the buildings. Having a room at the front of the hospital gave him a view of the Cumberland Mountains. He watched the setting sun paint ever-changing scenes from the shadows it cast until his peripheral vision caught motion in the doorway. He turned. A Bible waved up and down, soon followed by a bouncing figure. Benz, a grin from ear to ear, sprang to the foot of the bed, still waving the Bible.

"You must eat better than that if you expect to get out of here, Reverend." She eased around the bed, holding the Bible against her chest.

Methodically, he studied her, stricken by her youthful exuberance. She had on a summer dress that revealed a nice figure. Probably five-six, he reasoned. Next, he concentrated on her face, framed by a Dutch-boy haircut, the dark brown color enhancing her pure white skin. "You resemble my mother a lot, Doctor."

"Earlier I was too young. Do I now look old enough to resemble your mother?"

Heiter felt the warmth creep up to his scalp. He stammered momentarily. "I apologize. I meant you have the same pretty features and use them in your pleasant bedside manner." He bit his lower lip before he mumbled, "Sorry, that's too familiar. I mean no disrespect, Doctor."

"No apology needed. I came in here because I just saw your chest Xray and it looks fine. The E.R. Xray showed some blurring that made me suspect damage to your lung under the fractured ribs. Must have been some swelling because it is clear now. I'm happy for you."

*Charm, innocent youthfulness of a new physician, or is she just that way—like my mom*, Heiter debated. "Shouldn't you be in your white coat?" He grinned at her.

"I finished rounds late afternoon, ate dinner, rode the four miles to your church, and came back to bring the Bible." She thrust the book at him. "What's the monument in Baxter?"

"That's the Coal Monument, a symbol for all Harlan County folks. It's made of coal and commemorates the lives of the county miners," Milton said.

"They don't mine much coal now, do they?" Benz asked.

"No. The mines began closing in the early sixties. Harlan County had a population of around fifty-one thousand in '60. By the end of the century it had fallen to some thirty-five thousand," Milton said and put the Bible next to the food tray.

Benz pointed at the Bible. "Read for me the passage that prompted you to ask for a Bible." She sat on the edge of the bed, her perfume invading his nostrils.

Heiter took the Bible and flipped the pages until he came to the eighth chapter of Romans. He scooted up in the bed, glanced at her and hesitated when the conversation with the nurse flashed across his brain. Studying her eyes, he spoke without looking at the Bible, "The Spirit itself beareth witness with our spirit, that we are children of God: And if children, then heirs; heirs of God and joint heirs with Christ; if so be that we suffer with him that we may be also glorified together. For I reckon that the sufferings of this present time are not worthy to be compared with the glory which shall be revealed in us." As he spoke he patted the edge of the bed.

"You didn't need the Bible." Benz cast a coquettish face at Heiter and sat on the edge of the bed, one leg drawn up under the one touching the floor.

"Not for that scripture. This morning when I awoke from the head blow and the agent told me about the Caulders, I needed time alone with the Lord to ask his help. I needed the Bible then."

Benz frowned. "I'm somewhat of a Christian but I don't think God helps me so readily."

Heiter instinctively grabbed her hand. She stared in his eyes. "Doctor Benz, there is no such thing as a somewhat Christian. And He always answers—we don't always listen."

Susan leaned back using her arms as props. "Susan. If I call you Milton, you must call me Susan. And I've made some bad mistakes, that's what I meant." She paused, but Heiter cast a warm expectant look. Her blue-green eyes seemed to acquire a more greenish hue when the overhead light hit her green dress. She continued, "I've never been married...had an affair. He said he'd marry me after we lived together awhile. He split when I told him

I carried his offspring. I had an abortion—doesn't bother me. I wasn't going to raise a kid from some guy who used me, didn't love me—that's enough to make me 'somewhat,' don't you think?"

Startled by her frankness, Heiter put both his hands on her shoulders. "That's why Jesus died on the cross. That's why you are not somewhat—especially since you realize the mistake." He watched her eyes turn watery. She retrieved a hankie and dabbed them. He added, "We all make mistakes that are sins in God's eyes. He forgives, especially when we admit we were wrong and ask His forgiveness."

Her face melted. She grinned. "I wish my mother could hear those words. She has not forgiven me. Daddy told me to put it behind me."

"Tell you what. You help me through the guilt I harbor because two of my parishioners were burned alive…" His lip quivered ever so slightly. He hesitated to fight back the sorrow and continued, "in my house. They died for me and were innocent." He forced a weak smile. "I'll help you get personal and up close with the Lord."

Susan thrust a hand toward him, grabbed the one he offered, and shook it vigorously. "Now I've told you most of my wicked life. Your turn. Why aren't you married? Part of your religion?"

Heiter beamed, then let out a chuckle. "When I was in seminary, I went home early one day and found my wife in bed with a fellow seminarian, a friend. I haven't met anyone to obliterate the scars from that wound of six years ago—anyhow, this mission church keeps me fully occupied."

"Tell me. How is a mission church different? I want to understand how it can keep a handsome young preacher from finding companionship."

"That'd be a long story."

Susan pulled up a chair and sat. "I have hours. Teach me. It will help me understand these people."

"Appalachia has an interesting religious background, more like a distinct heritage. The mountain people often are called fundamentalists, but they aren't. At least not the way we mean when we call someone a fundie from today's world."

"From today's world?"

"Yes. You see, in a way, many of the folks in Appalachia haven't changed much for over a hundred and fifty years. Well, perhaps those in cities and county seats such as Harlan have, but even then not like in major cities as New York, Chicago or even Lexington. Now the mountain people are the same as 1910 when John Fox Jr. wrote his novels and stories about them. You ought to get some of John Fox's novels, they'll teach you more about these people than I ever will."

Susan took a pad from her purse and asked, "What are some of the titles? Maybe I can find some—library, or pull off the internet."

Milton scrunched up one side of his face, struggling to pull out titles. When Susan froze with pen poised over the pad, he said, "Oh, he's very popular here. Any local bookstore would have some. He's best known for *The Little Shepherd of Kingdom Come* and *A Knight of the Cumberland*. I particularly love his short story, 'The Army of the Callahan,' where he talks about Harlan's Home guard. Did you get all that down?"

Susan shook her head yes, so he continued, "Well, back to the mountain folk here in this area, especially when it comes to religion. They live by the Bible. They believe it's worse for them to break one of God's laws than to break a civil law. I'm boring you. That's enough for now. Come to my Sunday service and you'll get a good taste of other differences."

"I just may do that. You went to a Methodist seminary. Is Baxter Union Church Methodist?"

"No. For years it was the First Baptist Church. Seven years ago it became a mission church. Like many mission churches, it's a conglomerate: Presbyterian, Baptist, and Methodist. The pastor before me was Presbyterian. That is one way mountain churches may differ," Milton said.

"What are some other differences? If too foreign, I may pass."
Susan pushed out of the chair and sat on the edge of the bed again.

"Okay. First, they do not use bulletins. The service technically
starts at eleven. But at ten-forty many gather in the front of the
sanctuary. If we had a prayer room, it'd be in there. They give
forth with exhortative prayer with everyone praying their own
prayer out loud together. It almost sounds like a concert. I call it
a "concert prayer." The spooky thing is they always stop at the
same time. Gives me goose bumps. This is followed by singing
gospel hymns—anywhere from three to nine. A few churches have
the hymns 'lined' by a preacher or song leader. When hymns are
'lined,' a leader sings a line or stanza and the congregation immediately repeats it as sung. Another exhortative prayer will follow
with all joining in. Scripture reading, and then one or more exhortative preachers will give a sermon followed by testimonies or wit-
nesses to individuals' faith. After this an invitation is given to make
a decision for Christ, and a closing hymn is sung. Then there is a
blessing. We don't, but some churches even have front pews
reserved for those who are anxious about the condition of their
souls or who are under conviction of sin."

"Wow. That is different. Thanks for the lesson. It appears we
both have our work cut out for us." Susan slid off the bed and
stopped at the end of the bed. "I hope my confession hasn't colored
your opinion of my professional job? I've never told anyone those
secrets. On the other hand, I never had a pastor for a patient."

"You do remind me of my mother, Doctor. Your physician
skills are marvelous. We professionals ought to share personal
glitches."

"Good night, Milton. See you in the morning."

"Night, Doctor Benz. And thanks for sharing." He watched
her frown when he addressed her formally. She straightened,
turned and left. With her fading footsteps he thought, *This woman
acts more like mother than my twin sister. Strange. So open, or maybe
naïve, why tempted so easily into sin? No, I think she is a very trusting*

woman who has had little love at home—*I'll bet that's why she seems to need a friend.*

Sitting up in bed with the Bible resting on his lap, Milton found the scripture he had searched for and read from the fourth chapter of John. After he read the first part of the seventeenth verse that said, "The woman answered and said, I have no husband," he paused, for thoughts of Susan Benz crossed his mind. He narrowed his eyes and continued with the words of Jesus at the end of the seventeenth verse:

> *Thou hast well said, I have no husband: For thou hast had five husbands; and he whom thou now hast is not thy husband: in that saidst thou truly.*

Milton began to read further to refresh his memory of the words Jesus next spoke to the woman. *So much like Susan Benz,* he thought. *The world today isn't so...* Ringing interrupted his analogy. He stretched for the phone, picked up the receiver, watching the Bible fall to the floor.

"Milton, are you going to be alright?"

He smiled, for the voice was that of his twin sister Guthrie. "Bruises. I'm fine, Guthrie." he said.

"Concussion, broken nose, gash on your noggin and cracked ribs. Preachers have a weird concept of bruises," Guthrie said.

"How do you know all that? Hospital personnel aren't supposed to give out details. They usually say, 'Doing as well as can be expected.' I'm doing better than anyone expected."

"You made the Chicago Tribune two weeks ago, the business about your latest demonstration against Curewell Clinic. The mob broke windows to the fertility clinic and some got inside and trashed the place," Guthrie said.

"Five activists from out of town resorted to violence and others, locals who needed to vent, joined in. Two made it inside and broke up furniture in the reception area before the sheriff's men hauled them off to jail. When it started, I led my folks back to church," Milton said.

"I knew that, but the Daily News and TV had you as the ring-leader. The bombing of your house was on channel nine's evening news. They reported that 'Reverend Hitter' was alive but seriously injured. I called the hospital and they gave the message you told me, so I asked for your doctor's number," Guthrie said.

Milton lay back, pushed the receiver to his ear and stared at the ceiling. "So you spoke to Doctor Benz?"

"A few minutes ago. She seems nice. Said for a preacher you're easy to talk to, a good patient, even while you try to save her soul."

Milton couldn't suppress a laugh. Finally, he thought of a response, one that might derail what he knew would be Guthrie's next sisterly advice. "She's a pretty good doctor—for a woman." He grinned because from the silence he knew he had hit an old button.

"Oh yeah, I probably made her late so her fat husband had to take care of the snotty nosed kids—bet he didn't even start supper," Guthrie said.

"Got ya, Sis," Milton said. "She's not married. Actually, in all my holiness, I found her pretty. Reminds me of mother when she was younger. Hard for you to believe coming from a holy man, but I even noticed she has a great figure."

"Well, well. You are coming out of your cocoon, brother. I keep telling you that it isn't right for you to carry the hurts that Donna inflicted, your badge of martyrdom. Not healthy. You need a female companion…"

"Hold it. You're a good geneticist, a lousy psychologist," Milton said, his voice three decibels louder. "God sent me that thorn, my ex-wife's infidelity, as a message that I should devote my life to His work, unencumbered by a woman."

"Look at Billy Graham and Oral Roberts. They managed a family, passed on their commitment to offspring, very successful ones. And your favorite, Albert Schweitzer, was married. Besides, mother keeps telling me she wants you to get married and continue the Heiter name," Guthrie said.

"Forget it. I'm up to my ears trying to stop the Curewells and other companies like yours, Helpgenes, from murdering little beings. I don't have time to help a wife get over her sins. I do that all day long for men and women, and I'll try to do it for Benz. You and she think alike. She doesn't seem to think abortion is a sin," Milton said. He loosened his grip on the phone when his hand pained from strangling it.

"I can tell you aren't hurt very bad. And the concussion didn't knock any sense in your head. You still practice old-time religion. Get modern, brother," Guthrie said in a tone that let Milton know she teased him.

"I don't need a woman. I don't need modern religion. And I don't need advice from a geneticist," Milton grimaced because he let anger seep into the comment.

"Milton, I'm your sister. I want you to be happy. I worry all the time when I hear about the embryo factories, as you call them. Last month some of your more radical, old-time Christians shot the director of the fertility clinic in Los Angeles," Guthrie said.

"And here are my feelings, Sis. 'A new commandment I give unto you, That ye love one another; as I have loved you, that ye also love one another. By this all men know that ye are my disciples, if ye have love one to another.' John thirteen, verses thirty-four and thirty-five, Guthrie. I love you and Benz with Christian love as Jesus commanded. And I love you as a sister even though we don't see eye-to-eye on many things."

"That's nice, Milton. I love you, and I don't mean to tell you how to lead your life. I'm so proud of you. But having the doctor as just a friend would be good for your perspective when ministering to families," Guthrie said.

"Thanks, Sis. Tell that old man of yours I said hi."

"I shall. You be careful. Bye."

Milton said goodbye and placed the receiver in its cradle. He found the pillow remote and turned off the light. *Lord, I don't need female companionship. I want to feed your sheep. Please, keep me healthy, safe, and free of humanly distractions so I can follow in your son's footsteps.*

## TWO

Susan Benz showered with gusto, singing and dancing as she scurried around the apartment. *Strange man, but magnetic, his casual way of getting me to tell things I've never told anyone.* She read the morning paper while she ate her usual breakfast, an English muffin and black coffee. The heading of the right-hand column on the front page stopped her browsing: **BLAST AT PARSONAGE FROM BOMB** by Harry Zinger. She set her cup to the side and read:

> Reverend Milton Heiter is in fair condition after an attempt on his life. The pastor's own self-sacrificing nature saved his life as he let the Caulders, who lost their cabin in the deluge four days ago, use the church parsonage while the Reverend took quarters in a trailer once used for quarantine measures during the days of terrorism. The FBI is investigating the

bombing as a hate crime. Agent Tooms of the FBI believes that Heiter was the target because of his leadership in opposing Curewell Clinic, the local laboratory that produces and sells embryonic stem cells for research purposes. When asked if he agreed with the FBI's theory, Heiter said he doubted that was the only reason, because everyone knows that his protestations have been peaceful. True, at the march staged two weeks ago, when some of the demonstrators became violent, he called off the protest, taking most of the marchers back to the church. Perhaps other reasons exist; other parties angry with the Reverend. Curewell Clinic has been an economic boost for the area, and many families who were on the brink of poverty have benefited from the many enterprises spawned by the production of embryonic stem cells since their production and use for research became law eighteen months ago. Curewell sells thousands country-wide, some overseas. Regardless of the reason, the community in general is happy that the pastor is recovering rapidly. Most condemn such heinous acts as un-American, although one disgruntled citizen considers the Reverend's protestations as hypocritical because he heard Heiter is a product of in-vitro fertilization, created in a test tube as an embryo just as Curewell does."

Susan choked on a sip of coffee with the last quote. With great anticipation she hurried for the hospital. The muggy August air foretold of a scorcher. She carried the white coat over an arm until she was well within the hospital and approaching the nursing station. She changed her routine and went to Heiter's ward first. Not surprisingly, when she entered, he was reading the morning paper, his breakfast tray untouched.

"If you don't eat you'll never heal your wounds."

Glancing at his chart she had retrieved from the nurses' station, she continued. "Your vitals look good—for an embryo."

He dropped the paper, frowning until she broke into a huge grin as he said, "The uninformed hillbillies can't get it through their thick heads that in-vitro fertilization for the purpose of fulfilling God's commandment to multiply—in marriage—is moral, legal, and a joy for couples who otherwise could not have children. Now, making embryos for research purposes is not only a sin, it is murder, just like…"

She stared when Heiter's mouth froze open. He shrugged his shoulders and waved a hand. "I'm sorry. I wasn't throwing rocks."

Susan shifted from one foot to the other. She made a poor excuse for a smile and said, "That's okay. Abortion at nine weeks gestation isn't murder because the fetus isn't a being yet." She glared at him, daring him to disagree.

Heiter's face hardened, his brows narrowed when he squinted. "A neurosurgeon at the University of Missouri said that when the two DNAs join, making an embryo, a being exists. It has a soul. Abortion at any time after gestation is murder just like the murders Curewell Clinic does when they use embryos for research. Yeah, and worse, they experiment on beings, torture them."

Susan lowered her head while several thoughts flashed through her mind. Catholics have always thought abortions were murder. Yet until Roe versus Wade they didn't treat a embryo, fetus or still-born, as a person. They just incinerated them. They didn't act like they thought a person was there. In fact, Protestants did not really jump on the bandwagon until after Roe versus Wade. It's amazing how politics can affect church beliefs and practices. Abruptly, she looked up when she felt strong hands pull her up straight.

"Here, I want to be your friend, and I have offended you. I don't judge you, Susan."

Quickly, she decided to ignore his preaching. "You're pretty spry. I think you can be discharged after supper. I'll let the FBI know. They want to hover." She turned, making it as far as the door.

"I don't have any way to get home and I don't want the FBI driving me around—bad image for a preacher. Could you give me a lift?" The boyish smile melted her resolve.

A grin occupied her face. "Do you intend to go home in that?" She pointed to the light blue gown that went to his knees, showing off skinny legs.

"Mrs. Rawlins took my clothes that they removed in emergency and washed them last night. Fringe benefit for pastors, Susan. Will you? Please."

"I'll be here at six-thirty, Reverend." She said with frost on each word, whipped about and headed for the next patient's room, anxious to get to the office, sit, and sort through the competing emotions that tore at her tranquility. He sure is opinionated and sure of himself. He wasn't mean on purpose. He just didn't know any better, so why did I let it ruffle my feathers. Wasn't he really judging me? Or is it me feeling guilty? She chuckled as she opened the door to the clinic. *Two DNAs joining make a being? He can't give any science to prove that extreme view. But my cool reaction brought out a neat reaction. He does like me and so sudden. Cute guy—for a preacher.*

An impulse. At lunch Susan drove across the river to Walmart. In the section that held men's clothes, she beckoned to a man in Walmart attire. After she described Milton's physique, he told her she better bring the man in. When she told him the shirt was for Reverend Heiter, the guy beamed, soon replaced by a curious face.

"I'm the Reverend's doctor and plan to discharge him this evening. His clothes are a mess. I wouldn't want his flock to think he wasn't proper."

"Of course, Doctor. That's thoughtful. I read the article in the morning paper. Can't believe he has enemies."

The man showed Susan a rack, stating he was pretty sure that was Heiter's size. She chose a deep blue cotton short-sleeve shirt. During afternoon office hours Susan struggled to keep her mind on patients. Every now and then a thought broke through her medical cogitations. *A twin sister. So they must have implanted two in-vitro fertilized eggs and both grew. What a coincidence.*

Susan ate half of the cafeteria food, nervous about her coming task, nervous because he seemed too captivating and at the same time preaching at her. *Why did I tell him my past? His religion and my science won't mix. We'll never be close. He and I live two different lives,* she concluded.

When she entered his room he had his back to the door staring at the sun as it slipped below the mountains. He turned. She threw the shirt on the bed. "You are all signed out. Come. You can't wear that ragged, stained shirt." She went to the door and stopped. "Let's go to the treatment room. You'll feel more comfortable if I tape your broken ribs."

She walked toward the room, smiled at Rawlins and motioned to the treatment room. Rawlins followed them into the room. She took a roll of four-inch wide tape and showed Rawlins how long to cut strips. When Milton wrestled with the ragged shirt, she helped him remove it, and told him to sit on the exam table.

"Rawlins, you better shave the hair on the right side of his chest or he'll not appreciate our efforts when we remove the tape next week." While Rollins shaved his chest, Susan searched the cabinet until she spied the Tincture of Benzoin. Rollins painted the shaved side of Milton's chest with the sticky, brown liquid. Susan stared, admiring the lean but well-built figure. Methodically, she wrapped that side of his chest with five strips of adhesive tape, helped him pull on the new shirt, searching his eyes the whole time. They followed her moves and spoke trust, warmth, and what else?

Susan stepped back and folded her arms over her chest. "Take a deep breath."

Milton did as told and grinned. "Wow. That did the trick. No pain. Thanks, doctor. And thank you, Mrs. Rawlins. You'll get special attention in my prayers."

On the way to her car Susan instructed him about the care of his taped chest and the wound on the back of his head. The four-mile ride to the church was filled with nervous talk. She figured he was try-ing to fight off worry over the first sight of the demolished parsonage. *Why am I nervous?* she muttered as they pulled into the church parking lot. Milton got out and leaned against the car door, taking in the charred remains of his home. His eyes moved to the partially col-lapsed trailer that had been his temporary quarters. When his head dropped to his chest, Susan pushed beside him, put an arm around his waist. Tears ran down his cheeks.

"I want to help you through this tough time, Rev. Heiter. Please let me." Even as she said it, she had misgivings. *I need distance from this man. I don't understand him,* she thought.

He didn't answer. Instead he removed her arm from around his waist, held a hand and led her into the church. They marched down the center aisle. A quick glance told her it probably held no more than 150 people. The carpet softened their footsteps so she imagined they could hear her heart beat. Milton stopped at the altar rail, kneeled, his look telling her to do the same. He dropped her hand and rested both elbows on the altar rail, folded his hands, and stared at the stained-glass figure of Jesus, filling half the end wall of the narthex.

"Gracious loving father, thank you for being with us through this tragedy. Hold the Caulders in your loving arms and send your spirit down to comfort their family and our community. Lord, thank you for hearing my prayers. Thank you for sending me a car-ing doctor in my time of need. Help her as she so skillfully goes about taking care of your sheep. Lord, help the people of this com-munity to open their hearts to her and to trust her. Lord, I hurt and ask for your wisdom and guidance. You know I abhor violence, and yet as I stand as an advocate for the defenseless would-be children, violence is all around; even injury and death. Lord, let me be an instrument of your peace, but also let me be your minister of rec-onciliation with a message that will not only stop the violence but also the killing of embryos. For it's in Jesus's name, the Prince of Peace, I pray. Amen."

He turned and helped her stand before she could wipe the tears. She made a feeble grin and stepped back. "You want to be my patient after what I told you last night?"

"Of course, you've done a good job getting me back to my flock," he said.

She turned and faced him. "Tell me about your family."

"You know my sister and I are products of in-vitro fertilization thirty years ago." He sat in the first pew and waited for her to sit beside him. "My father was a brilliant physicist at Argonne National Laboratories outside Chicago. But his sperm count was so low the only way they could conceive was by IVF. They implanted in Mom's uterus two of her eggs they had fertilized in a petri dish. Both took, grew to be my sister Guthrie and me. She's a geneticist. I love her but we have differing opinions about embryonic stem cells being used for research, especially produced solely for that purpose."

Susan was captivated by the story. "She's a scientist. The age-old fight between science and religion continues." When he screwed up the corner of his mouth, searching her face, she decided to change the subject. "Tell me about your mother. Your father sounds like a genius."

"Was—he was killed when terrorists blew up two buildings at Argonne in oh-three. Mother is pretty—like you—and a charmer. She has a way of attracting the emotions, the attention of those she meets. You are so much like her. Guthrie is like Pa, brilliant, cool, and calculating."

Susan sat spellbound, the dark chapel going unnoticed until Milton went over to a cabinet in the corner, took some matches and lit the candles at each end of the altar. The interlude gave her time to make a decision. "Maybe it's IVF. You see, my father wanted a child so badly but had mumps when a boy. Mother is beautiful, a model and actress—not Hollywood—in theater. She didn't want a child to mess up her figure or interfere with her ambitions. Daddy's the top neurosurgeon at Northwestern. He…"

"Doctor Samuel Benz, the renowned professor of neuro-surgery at Northwestern. He took the famous Loyal Davis's place."

"Yes. Poor man owned the world but couldn't have the thing he wanted most."

"So they adopted you."

"Close. They bought a fertilized egg and paid a woman to be the surrogate. That way mother's career wasn't jeopardized." She noticed she was twisting her hands, so she sat on them.

"But they raised you well—a magnificent doctor, caring, warm, quite bright." Milton moved close, looking deep into her eyes.

His eyes were questioning as if he knew the answer, so she added, "Daddy saw me every day of my life until I went to college. A nanny raised me. I have few memories of mother."

"How do you feel about yourself? IVF kid and product of a surrogate pregnancy, raised by a loving father and a nanny."

Susan snapped her head up, and noticing the concerned look, knew this perceptive man realized he had hit a sensitive spot. She managed a smile and thrust a hand palm first when his mouth opened. "Sorry for my knee-jerk response. Haven't ever been quizzed so directly." She fiddled with her hair, crossed her legs, buying time. "I'm stalling because I have never verbalized my feelings."

"I'm sorry. We have already shared secrets, personal ones. Don't answer if it makes you uncomfortable." His posture, more than the weak smile, told her he cared.

"I often wondered if the lack of love from my mother—maybe too much from my father—knocked down my barriers toward sex before marriage. I don't believe in it. I didn't believe it was right unless you married, but as it turned out, it was a sin, so I naturally felt ashamed, guilt, a poor self-image." She looked at his eyes, grimaced and continued. "I reasoned that blaming Mother's lack of affection, maybe rejection of me, was an excuse. I was rational, knew it was sinful and what it could lead to, and did. So I am totally responsible."

"Have you talked to the Lord in this way?"

"No. I was taught...I believe he knows what's in my heart, my silent prayers to him about the mess I made."

She watched Milton squirm. He beamed. "You are a phenom-enon. He does, and that's why you've done so well."

"I'm not so certain about that. But one bad reflex since I let myself be taken advantage of by a man has been quick and com-plete. Since the last fall and the abortion I haven't let any male get close, raise my interests."

"Fear, Susan?"

"Fear of what?"

"I don't know. Fear of being caught off guard, of being hurt, of offending your God." She watched him stroke his chin, obvi-ously now the one wrestling with a tough question. "Excellent question," he said.

"I never thought about that one either. You know I wish I had you to talk to six years ago. I should have considered such things. I believe I felt I would never find someone who loved me, who wanted my companionship, raise a family. I put on cynical armor."

"The twin purposes of marriage according to Genesis one and two are for companionship and procreation. While you may not have verbalized it then, your explanation says that you believed precisely what God wants. Psalm 129 says the marriage vows affirm the purpose of marriage. The man and woman are now able to pursue holiness together in the church, knowing God is pursuing them. Men and women were not created to pursue holiness alone but to be companions pursuing union with God, with other Christians in the church. We are created never to be alone, but have each other to be supported, nurtured, and encouraged by the fellowship of the church. We in contemporary America tend to be too individualistic, competitive, and distrust-ing. That's why I love it here in Appalachia, for we still live in a village where everyone knows and looks out for everyone else— that is until recently."

"You make it sound easy. I guess we humans make it diffi-cult." She felt at ease as if a weight had been lifted from her shoul-ders. "Thanks for hearing me. I feel better."

"I do that as part of my ministry…"

She interrupted by blurting, "I'm your doctor, and here I end up on your counseling couch." She felt uneasy again, let her chin fall on her chest until a warm hand raised her head.

"No, Susan. Last night after you left I made a decision, reinforced after this conversation, that I would help you with the sin, the one you deny, the one that subconsciously forces you to make poor compensatory adjustments. The way I ask questions about a person's concerns comes from doing that in my ministry for years. You see, I agree with John Wesley, the founder of Methodism. He said, 'The only purpose for the church is to be an infirmary to heal sin sick souls.' But asking you goes way beyond that, it came from a desire to help a friend."

The furrows at the corner of his eyes, their laser look made a shiver creep up her spine. "Well," Susan blurted, hesitated and with emphasis on Reverend, continued, "Reverend Heiter, we may be a couple IVF kids, but you have it wrong. I have no repressed guilt about the abortion. And I am quite aware of the battle between science and religion." She rose and turned away from him. "Our differences started way back in 300 B.C. when the priests held that the earth was the center of the universe. Aristotle, the father of science, concluded from his astronomy observations that the sun was the center of the universe. They made him change his conclusion."

Milton rose and moved close. In the dim light of the sanctuary she could see his eyes widen, dancing while he said, "Copernicus, the Polish astronomer, around 1500 A.D. concluded the same as Aristotle. The church had him thrown in jail. However, Susan, soon after that, under pressure from the findings of Galileo and Newton, the church acquiesced and agreed with the scientists that the sun was the center of the universe."

Susan hesitated while he blew out the candles. Then she said, "But the church and science wars surfaced in modern times—if you accept 1925 as modern. The Scopes monkey trial in Dayton, Tennessee pitted science, evolution, against religion and creation. I believe science won that one also."

Milton took her arm and they walked toward the front door. "You mean Clarence Darrow won the debate. See God made science and makes scientists, so William Jennings Bryan should have said that God made evolution part of his plan, so that man wouldn't become extinct like the dinosaurs. But, since that popularized debate, science has shown that the link Darrow used to show that man came from a monkey was a fraud."

"And what do you say about the big bang that formed the earth?" Susan opened the door and spotted a car parked next to hers.

Milton stepped outside and turned to her. "The gases that made the big bang, where did they come from?" He smiled. "If you want to believe the earth was formed by a big bang, someone made the gases, the conditions to form the earth, very precise conditions for the bang. God did it. He formed the universe that way, if you scientists need some scientific jargon to help you believe."

Susan caught the drift of his reasoning. "Do you know of any scientific proof that when two DNAs join, a being is formed? Did that neurosurgeon from Missouri offer any scientific evidence?"

"Do you have any scientific evidence that proves the existence of a being at any time during gestation?"

Milton had spoken her thoughts so she answered, "Touche. Science can't prove that, Milton."

"Precisely. Science can't prove the seat of the soul either. These things are the essence of faith just as the existence of God." He pointed to a car parked next to hers. "FBI car. Tooms said he would see that I had protection."

Susan waved at a figure that came out of the shadows on the side of the church. The man waved back and leaned against the car. The passenger's door opened and a stranger climbed out. Both men approached them.

Tooms spoke before she could greet him. "This is Hank Abel, my associate from Washington. Hank, meet Doctor Susan Benz and her patient, the Reverend Milton Heiter."

Susan said hello while Milton shook Abel's hand. He was Milton's height with a lean face and coal black hair. A mustache sat below a long nose. The black eyes sat in dark sockets, giving the man a most intense look. He stood stiff as a rod and acted more formal than Tooms. She figured him to be fifteen years younger than the fifty-five year-old Tooms. The man went behind the FBI car, opened the trunk and returned with a sleeping bag and a small backpack.

"Hank will sleep in the back of the church, if that's okay with you, Milton," Tooms said.

Abel stepped closer, glanced at Susan, making a stiff smile. The moon shone on his face as he turned toward Milton. His countenance made her say under her breath, "Stone face."

"Reverend, I will be unobtrusive. In fact, in the morning I will be in different attire, probably dressed like a workman. On any given day, I may dress similar to any of a variety of different trades." He inched back toward Tooms while he added, "I will do my best not to interfere with your daily routine. But you might as well know that I don't agree with your behavior, the marches, or your phony church life. My job is to keep you from harm, and I will do that, even though at times you may not like my presence. Just remember, I am here for your protection."

Susan watched Milton, his face a grayish blur with the moon shining from behind. His facial gestures were readable; he wasn't pleased with the message or the man spewing it at him. "I find this whole business a bit of an over-reaction, Tooms. And I prefer that the FBI not sleep in my church. Try the remains of the trailer. I'll bet you've slept in worse places during surveillance."

Tooms turned to Abel. "Good idea the reverend has. Besides, you won't be sleeping that much."

Susan caught the frown before Milton walked her to her car. When they neared the cars, she turned and waved to Tooms and Abel. She climbed behind the wheel and looked up at Milton. "Call me. I need to remove those stitches and the tape next week. And we need to continue this debate."

Milton said he'd call. As she pulled away she heard Milton ask Tooms where he intended to sleep.

The drive to her apartment on the other side of Harlan seemed shorter than usual, sped along by the troublesome thoughts brought out the past two hours in the church and the cool meeting the four had in the dark. *I guess the FBI have to remain stiff and aloof. Now Milton, was he being a professional preacher or did he interrogate me because he likes me? He's cunning, getting me to debate science and religion, leading me to dissect faith, probably wants me to examine mine. If it'll help, I'll discuss it further. I don't want to make any more mistakes, be hurt, or lonely.*

# Chapter
# THREE

Reverend Milton Heiter scanned the church. Every pew was crowded with motley-appearing folk, some in ragged shirt and Levi's, or worn dress while others were in suit and tie or fancy dress, all in their Sunday-go-to-meeting finest. Not an unusual collection in recent weeks, but the people standing shoulder to shoulder against the sidewalls and at the back were intimidating. Worse, though, was the need of a microphone. Normally, he did not need any assistance because his baritone voice carried well. Often he had been told that with the timbre of his voice he could have been the next Tom Brokaw. Milton straightened to his full six-one height and shot a glance past those in the rear and through the open door. The view quickened his pulse, the reason for the need of a microphone. The parking lot was covered with people, TV apparatus, radio microphones and reporters, pad in hand, all anxious to catch his message. As he shuffled the papers he scrutinized those in the small chapel, smiling at one, nodding at another, but searching for a special face, Susan's.

After he thanked them for their prayers, for their concern, and for their elbow grease applied Saturday in building a new parsonage, they smiled and shuffled in the pews. Nodding, he said, "I had heard about 'Mountain Ethic,' but now I have seen it in action. The way the Caulder kin and friends—the way the whole community pulled together—bulldozed the burned parsonage off the property and helped put up a new home for their pastor is validation of your faith. Yes, you truly walk by faith and live by love. You truly rally around one another in times of crisis. Thank you! My special thanks go to the parents and kin of Mr. and Mrs. Abraham Caulder, who even after suffering such a tragic loss, still came out and helped rebuild the parsonage. God bless you." His lip quivering, he turned slightly and looked at the stained glass window, the figure of Jesus. An awed silence fell over the chapel. So much that one could hear the background noise from the parking lot.

"Let's have a moment of silence for our fallen brethren, Mr. and Mrs. Abraham Caulder." He used the interlude to take control of his emotions. "Silently, let each of us pray for Mr. Caulder's parents and for brother Jethroe." He waited. Only the rustling of leaves carried by a breeze found his ears. He opened his Bible to Psalm 139 and, staring at the front pews, moving his gaze to the back ones, said, "Now hear the word of the Lord from Psalm one hundred and thirty-nine, verses thirteen to sixteen:

> *For you created my inmost being; You knit me together in my mother's womb; I praise you because I am fearfully and wonderfully made; your works are wonderful, I know full well. My frame was not hidden from you when I was made in the secret place. When I was woven together in the depths of the earth your eyes saw my unformed body. All the days ordained for me were written in your book before one of them came to be. How precious to me are your thoughts, O God. How vast is the sum of them."*

Heiter looked up from the Bible and said, "Please rise for the reading of the Gospel. The Gospel is from Luke, the seventeenth chapter, verses one to three:

> *Jesus said to his disciples, 'Things that cause people to sin are bound to come, but woe to the person through whom they come. It would be better for him to be thrown into the sea with a millstone tied around his neck than for him to cause one of these little ones to sin, so watch yourselves.'*

May the Lord add his richest blessing to the reading of His holy word. Please be seated."

Carefully, Milton set the stage for his mission that Sunday by describing what he saw and heard as he stepped out of the trailer, his temporary quarters, to afford the Caulder couple a home after the creek washed away part of their cabin. He told them his emotions when he heard they lost their lives and the heavy heart he felt when the FBI told him it was a bomb meant to frighten him, that the demon-possessed culprits—the FBI already knew that two set off the blast—hadn't known about the propane tanks on the back porch. They found a grimy straw hat and tire tracks of a small truck on the road that ran along the side of the church property.

A small clamor arose from some pews when he told them that he was in college when terrorism first hit the U.S. and that the terrorist attempts since the global war were no different than the blast that took the lives of the Caulders. "I was frightened at first, then grief hit me, then anger. I know the FBI will catch those two sick individuals, and those who paid them to do such a cowardly act. Now I am not afraid. So with this message I am going to tell those terrorists why they are wrong. They will lose because this nation has reverence for life, and because as our scriptures of the morning bear witness to us, God will not tolerate the taking of human life from the time of conception through old age. Yes, it would be better to have a millstone tied around our neck and to be thrown into the depths of the sea than to sin by taking the life of one of God's children. Yes, as an embryo in a petri dish, in the womb, or child-hood or as adults. We shall not kill, so watch yourselves."

Methodically, he reviewed three topics that on the surface might make foreigners think the United States did not have rever-ence for life; in-vitro fertilization, surrogate pregnancy, and use of spare embryos or production of embryos for research purposes. Murmurs spread throughout the chapel. Next, he briefly outlined the legal actions beginning with President Clinton, and then President Bush's action to allow use of stem cell lines, and later his veto of the Congressional bill that allowed the use of spare embryos from in-vitro fertilization. Emphatically, he described the law signed by President Campbell that allowed production of embryos for research.

He threw an arm at the congregation. "You are responsible for that embryo factory, the killing house of tiny beings, so watch your-selves." In unison the figures froze in the pews and frowns grew, some replaced with disbelief and others a hint of anger. "You, me, all of the public let the media pull off their greatest anti-religion campaign since the day they stopped school prayer. They say they always give both sides of issues. My brothers and sisters, listen. Watch yourselves. Hear the sophistry, the distortion, the alleged evidence in favor of their hidden agenda. So the politicians passed this demonic legislation, turned terrorists on the smallest of beings, because the polls showed the majority of Americans thought it all right to produce embryos for stem cell research. After all they might, possibly they could, hopefully they will cure diabetes, repair spinal injuries, and help us cure cancer, heart disease, and any other disease that evokes our deepest emotions, so watch your-selves. The people who responded to the pollsters were educated by these anti-Christ media. What could the spineless politicians do? They wanted to get reelected."

Milton paused, opened his black coat and extracted a hankie from an inside pocket, all the while studying the faces. The harsh message had an eclectic effect, disturbing many, and bringing forth smiles on some. "In the coming weeks I will bring you messages that will show you what the Bible says about these issues. In the meantime, I will continue the war on terrorists who murder the smallest of beings. Am I afraid?" He smiled and opened the Bible to the mark he had placed. "I read from Mathew ten, verse twenty-eight:

> *And fear not them which kill the body, but are not able to kill the soul: but rather fear him which is able to destroy both soul and body in hell, so watch yourselves."*

His penetrating eyes slowly roamed around the congregation as he closed the Bible. "Let us pray. O Lord! Let us ever be vigilant and protect our freedoms as Americans. Lord, we denounce all forms of terrorism—especially terrorism against the small and defenseless. Help us, O God, to watch ourselves and be sure we lead no one astray to participate in the killing of the innocent. In Jesus's name we pray. Amen."

Milton felt a glow, a deep inner warmth. He raised his arms slowly as he said, "Please rise and sing 'Child of Blessing, Child of Promise' as our closing hymn."

Milton began the hymn in a deep baritone, chanting voice. The people responded to each line most sincerely, until verse three and then, strangely, about half of the congregation quit singing. Some wept openly while others seemed to become angry. He sang:

"Child of joy, our dearest treasure. God you are, from God you come. Back to God we humbly give you; live as one who hears Christ's name."

Suddenly people began to make their way to the altar rail, sad, kneeling in prayer. Milton continued singing the last verse:

"Child of God your loving parent, Learn to know whose child you are. Grow to laugh, and sing, and worship and love God more than all. Amen and Amen."

Milton paused and looked solemnly out over the congregation, finally focusing on those kneeling at the altar. Raising his right hand slowly, he said, "Receive the blessing. Rise, go in peace and serve the Lord. Amen."

It seemed several minutes before the first parishioners stood and walked up the aisle. Milton exited the back door, dashed around to the front and shook the hands of the departing folks. With the crowd gone, the media surrounded Milton. He surveyed the mass of people, microphones thrust at him and cameras aimed in his direction. To his right he spied Zinger, notepad in hand. In back his vision caught the smiling face of Susan. She gave a subtle wave with the fingers of a hand raised above the herd. He smiled broadly until the first question prodded his defenses.

"Reverend Heiter, why do you blame the media, accuse us of being anti-Christ?"

Milton began to perspire in the hot midday sun. Loosening his tie and removing his jacket gave him time to design a metered answer. Further time came from his surprising query. "You ask me personal questions of my beliefs, what I live by, what I suffer and fight for. You know my name. Please give me the same courtesy. I don't know you." He forced his most charming smile and continued. "I know Mr. Zinger of our paper, and I see my doctor is present, Doctor Susan Benz." He jabbed a long index finger in their direction.

The man who had asked the question waved a wad of papers and said, "I am Mike Crouse of the Washington Post."

"Mr. Crouse, I know some papers are more fair than others in giving the Word equal time with political correctness. I don't read the Washington Post so I do not blame anyone individually. However, if the shoe fits, put it on. Don't be a chameleon to your readers."

"What television shows do you like? What do you read beside the Bible, Reverend?" A female voice from his right shrieked.

"Sorry, I missed your name, m'am." Milton tried to find the source of the utterance.

"Katherine Hardin of NBC."

"I don't have a television set. I read the Harlan Dailey practically every day, and I can tell you that the shoe fits Mr. Zinger. He

writes like an antichrist. His sense of fairness, of balanced reporting, died along with the horse and buggy." He looked in Zinger's
direction, smiled and waved.

"Milton," the same squat man pushed his way through the
crowd and stopped near him. Talking to the other reporters, he
said, "I'm Zinger of the local paper and young Heiter here is an
anachronism. With his head in the sand he fights modern tech-
nological advances with antiquated methods. He is not a modern
Christian, and has no understanding of tolerance or political correctness."

Milton sidestepped closer to Zinger, placed an arm around
his shoulder. "Mr. Zinger, that shoe fits me perfectly and is very
comfortable. My old-fashioned weapons to fight scientific
advances allow no quarter for political correctness, or tolerance of
those who harbor and justify sin for political correctness." He
waved his Bible over his head. "My weapons come from this book,
from the words of Jesus Christ. He is an anachronism. He is antiquated. He is my savior. Invite Him. He'll be yours, too. Even
yours, Zinger!"

For the next half hour the trick questions, the veiled accusa-
tions, and the verbal traps failed to change Milton's resolve to
answer with the word from the book he waved at questioners.

"Thank you all for coming to Harlan. These mountain people
live by the Bible. They live antiquated lives, anachronistic existence,
but will follow Jesus's teaching in spite of the tools the outside tries
to thrust on them. Yet, they will be kind to strangers, even to a
fault. Stay and visit with them, and come to church service next
week. I'll convince you that the Bible speaks to today's social and
political problems."

Susan burst through the crowd and accompanied him into the
church. Inside, she led him to the front pew, sat him down, and
went to the pulpit, returning with the glass of water he kept there
during sermons. While he downed the water, enjoying the cool,
soothing effect on his parched throat, she asked him to explain the

sin of surrogate pregnancy, and how it relates to the Bible. Her biting words were spoken in a tense manner. Charming, he thought.

"Susan, I know that you are the product of a surrogate pregnancy. In actuality, you did not sin. However, your father and mother and the surrogate sinned."

"You seem so quick to judge other people's actions. I do not understand how you can so easily condemn my family. I asked you to explain the sin of surrogate pregnancy, not to attack my family personally," Susan exclaimed.

"I am sorry. I did not mean to attack your family. It's just that your parents and the surrogate repeated an ancient activity. Do you remember the biblical story in Genesis of Abraham, Sarah, and Sarah's maidservant, Hagar?"

Appearing to be in deep thought, Susan said, "Yes. Didn't Sarah convince Abraham to take Hagar, and she gave birth to Ishmael? What has that got to do with a surrogate mother?"

"Everything," said Milton, "The reason is different because Sarah desperately wanted a child and your mother did not. Yet, as your folks used a woman to incubate you, so Abraham and Sarah used Hagar to have a son, Ishmael. What really makes the story ironic and tragic is that when Sarah had Isaac, she had Abraham banish Ishmael. But God watched out for them and two great peoples came from Isaac and Ishmael, the Jews from Isaac and the Arabs from Ishmael. Think about it, the tensions in the world between the Jews, Christians, and the Arabs. The terrorist wars by extreme Islamic terrorists, the descendents of Ishmael against Israel and those who support her. Even the continued strife between Palestinians and Jews over Jerusalem and the Holy Land can be traced back to Abraham and Sarah's decision to use Hagar as a surrogate mother." Milton ran a hand through his hair and grinned at Susan. "Boy, did I get carried away? Please forgive my meanderings. But do remember. It is not your sin. You are not responsible for the actions of your parents and the surrogate."

"You're going a little too fast for me now. We are both products of IVF. Your father's sperm fertilized your mother's egg in a petri dish, and my father purchased an embryo, an egg fertilized by some man's sperm that fertilized a woman's egg. The embryo was implanted in another woman's uterus. If he hadn't purchased that embryo, it would have been used for research, so according to your belief, he saved a life." Susan paused to let Milton answer, but he seemed deep in thought. "He told me he didn't know names but picked an embryo whose male donor was a scientist and the woman pretty and a charmer."

Milton beamed. "I am looking at the product of that selection. Genetics held true."

Susan blushed and said, "So the surrogate was just an incubator, added nothing—well, she kept an embryo alive. If she went beyond nurturing and decided to keep the baby for herself, that sure would have messed up things. Surrogacy doesn't seem so bad."

Milton waved a hand at her. "Susan, please, I am not trying to attack you personally. Just think about it a minute before..."

Susan interrupted, "Oh! You are going to bring up that it's not natural—that natural law stuff."

"No, no," he said. "That's a whole different issue. It's kinda like adultery when the father's sperm goes into another woman, not his wife. Remember, I said the twin purposes of marriage were companionship and procreation—where the married couple is intimate, there for each other throughout the entire pregnancy. That's impossible with a surrogate. It should not surprise us when surrogates not only feel and bond with the baby, but they even want to keep it. The issue is that a woman other than the wife is impregnated, and the couple for the whole nine months is unable to bond with the fetus."

"I'm still confused. Who sinned? It wasn't my father's sperm or my mother's egg—she wouldn't have her pretty belly violated—maybe she didn't want half the kid to be her."

"They caused the surrogate to sin, so they sinned. Why didn't they just adopt a kid and avoid that?"

Susan shrugged her shoulders. "Guess that would have been cleaner—adoption. But my father wanted to be involved emotionally throughout the surrogate's pregnancy in spite of your contention that surrogacy eliminates bonding."

"Never thought about that. Yes, I can see him fretting, checking on the progress of the pregnancy, the health of the surrogate, telling her the things she must do to have a healthy baby."

She poked a finger on his chest. "But no matter, that means I was born in sin. And I know I have sinned, some terrible, in my life."

"Haven't we all sinned, Susan? Your parents and the surrogate's decision and act were not your sin." He pulled her off the pew and, leading her to the door, added, "Jesus died on the cross so we don't have to carry the guilt around with us. He knows what is in our hearts. And I perceive you have a pure heart." They had reached the front steps. "Isn't the parsonage beautiful? That's the religion of mountain people. Many who aren't members showed up yesterday to build a structure better than the old one. They may be poor by city standards, but they are caring and generous, loving."

"I best go. I have reading to catch up."

Milton turned and stared down into her eyes. "I am so happy you were present today. It bolstered my courage, so I want to take you to visit the Caulders. You'll learn some things about these people and how they live."

Susan grabbed a hand and marched him to her car. "I'll drive. You navigate."

Milton threw his tie and coat in the back seat. He pointed to the mountain. "We go toward the Cumberland Mountains on 421 for about six miles before turning on a narrow gravel road that leads to a small meadow beside a babbling brook. Some day I'll take you there."

Five miles up the winding asphalt he motioned for her to pull over toward a narrow rocky driveway. Susan slowed, and turning onto the rocky way, jammed on the brakes.

"This the road to your special place?" She had seen the incline of the drive that led into a stream.

"This is the drive to the Caulder house." He pointed to their left. "That decrepit bridge is a walkway. When there's been a big rain up the mountain the creek is swollen and too deep to drive to the house, so they park here and cross over the bridge. See the shack, mostly fallen in the creek. That was the home of the couple burned to death in the parsonage. We are going to pay our respects to his parents."

Susan eased the car into the stream, barely a foot deep, and ascended the far bank. "Where are her parents?"

"Good question. Frequently, when the man marries he and the wife move in with his parents. Her parents are dead, killed by that terrorist attack up in Virginia in 2006. A young son, Jethroe, lives at home."

Susan stopped the car in front of the weatherworn gray house, some thirty feet from the creek. One corner of the porch sagged, an ancient, rusty refrigerator perched precariously nearby. Next to it sat a cumbersome looking sofa, its cover worn, revealing springs in at least two places. Milton climbed out as the torn screen door opened. A lanky, bent man in bib overalls stopped at the edge of the porch.

"Welcome, Preacher Man. Come in—with yer lady friend."

"Mr. Caulder, this is Doctor Benz. She got me healthy enough to come pay my respects." As he spoke a round figure appeared in the doorway. Straight, gray hair hung over her shoulders. A flour-sack dress hung over her protuberant belly straight to the top of her dirty, worn brown shoes.

"Needn't do that, Preacher. We got yer message. Thanks fer all the prayers. Come in and have a bite. Folks here abouts brung us so much we'll never eat it all."

She shuffled back inside. The bent-over figure hobbled in and they followed. Milton sat in a creaky wooden chair and motioned for Susan to sit across from him. Mr. Caulder sat at one end. Mrs.

Caulder set a piece of apple pie and a glass of cider in front of each. She eased into a wobbly old wooden chair.

"Where's Jethroe, sir? Haven't seen him for a while," Milton said.

"He been hangin' out in the woods, poutin' since the explosion. If he seed you 'ens, he'll pop in."

Milton thanked them for helping the mountain folk build the new parsonage, and told them what a blessing Susan had been to the community since her arrival. The back screen door slammed shut and Jethroe hovered by the door. He had a square build, arms huge like a weight lifter. His wide-set black eyes were framed by bushy, black hair. He had at least two days of stubble with flaring nostrils and thin lips. Jethroe's demeanor and slouched posture gave the initial impression that he wasn't too smart. Milton knew better. He bounded out of his chair and embraced Jethroe. The man's eyes lit up and his face reddened.

"Jethroe, the folks built me a new parsonage."

"I seed it from the woods this morning, Preacher." He leaned against the chipped, gray porcelain sink and Milton returned to his chair. Susan watched intently, eating her pie in nibbles.

"Delicious pie, Mrs. Caulder," she offered. Mrs. Caulder nodded.

"Mr. Caulder. With the new parsonage and my cracked ribs I sure could use Jethroe." He watched Jethroe's head snap up, a grin on his lean face.

"He don't know much, couldn't be much help," the man said, staring at his glass of cider.

"Pa, I could do some of the chores like here. Please?"

"I can't pay lots but I expect to pay for his work, Mr. Caulder," Milton said and smiled at Jethroe.

"Woman, what ya think?"

"If'n the preacher needs help and thinks Jethroe can help, seems fine to me." She surveyed her son. "But you gonna tidy up if'n you goin' be around a preacher's house, son."

"I will, Mom. When do I start?" Jethroe rocked from one foot to the other, his glee uncontainable.

"Show up at nine in the morning, Jethroe." Milton stood and Susan did also. At the door he thanked them for the pie and cider and for letting Jethroe help.

Once Susan had maneuvered the car onto the road and headed back down the mountain, she quizzed him about Jethroe. Milton told her that the dull-appearing man was actually fairly bright, just unschooled. While he answered, he smiled to himself when he spotted Tooms's car in the side-view mirror. But the smile gave way to a frown when he realized that the FBI had entered his personal life.

Susan stopped in front of the parsonage and Milton climbed out. Through the window he said, "I'll call you in a few days."

"Better if I call you. I still need to take out those stitches at the end of the week."

Before her car disappeared from view, a black Buick pulled into the church parking lot. Tooms climbed from behind the wheel, shut the door, and strode to Milton. He was in shirtsleeves. Before speaking he removed heavy sunglasses, stuffed them in a shirt pocket. His hair was windblown, but he seemed relaxed.

"That would be the Caulders you visited. Good education for the young doc." He stiffened suddenly, brought his right arm before his eyes and with the other hand poked a small button on the side of a wristwatch. "Here, Hank. He...they're fine. Didn't see anything."

Bewildered at first by the monologue, Milton searched Tooms's face. His eyes spotted an earpiece, flesh colored and hardly perceptible. Tooms saw Milton's eyes rest on the ear. He reached in a pants pocket and removed a small black object. He pushed a switch on the side with his thumb, removing the earpiece with the other. "I found the rat-trap house where that Mort and Ezrah live." The voice coming from the object sounded like the mechanical voice of the computerized radio reports, so Milton mumbled, "Who?" The voice continued so Tooms mouthed, "Hank."

"I caught them alone. Don't know where the mom was, so I confronted them with the evidence, the straw hat, and the tire tracks. They denied them being theirs, so I told them DNA from hair and sweat matched DNA from blood samples the hospital had on Ezrah and the road tracks matched those on their old truck."

Tooms raised his arm and spoke into the watch. "Did that rattle them?"

"Not Mort. But Ezrah began to sob and lashed out at Mort. Anyhow, I wanted to give a brief report now because I have some concern I may have been followed up the hollow where they live. They confessed some middle-aged man gave them a thousand dollars to blow the preacher's house. Told them only to scare the preacher, to be sure he wasn't in the kitchen so he wouldn't get hurt. They didn't know about the propane tanks. But their contact did because he stressed the importance of putting the bomb precisely under the kitchen window."

"Hank, I'm with Milton." He faced Milton. "The tanks near that location?"

"Just a foot to the left on the back porch," Milton said.

"I caught that, Max." The words came from the object. "I didn't bring them in. Made a deal—that Mort is no dummy—that if they would help us find their contact, the court would go light on them because they didn't know about the tanks, didn't mean any harm to people."

Tooms surveyed the surroundings, a full 360 degrees. "We better move quickly, since you suspect someone may have followed you. I'll cover here tonight. See you in the morning." He pushed the side button on the watch and replaced the object along with the earpiece.

The two men went to the church office, where Tooms reviewed the FBI's findings and their next steps. He leaned an elbow on the desk and said, "Okay, time for you to educate me, since my original task was to check out the activities at Curewell Clinic. You're a product of in-vitro fertilization, so I bet you know more than most lay people."

"When I was in college my parents told me Guthrie and I were products of IVF. The first attempts at IVF began in the mid

60

seventies and in 1978 the first, baby Louise Brown, was born. So when sis and I were born two years later, it was quite an event."

"Twins. I imagine that was a surprise." Tooms slipped off his shoes and removed his tie.

"Back then only 10 percent of fertilized eggs implanted in the woman's uterus went on to term, so they usually put in three, if they had gotten that many. If they implanted two, 30 percent of the time one was carried to term and if three, one was produced 36 percent of the time. Now and then, as with mom, two implanted embryos went to term."

Tooms moved to the edge of his chair. "Your parents obviously were happy having twins. What about those who weren't so thrilled? Or what if three grew and they didn't want but two, or maybe only one?"

"Not obviously. If they didn't want two—I have no idea what my parents thought about the extra surprise. But they would not have had mom go through abortion. Others have been upset and the woman undergoes what is called a partial abortion."

"How has the business changed since those early days?"

Milton disappeared into the bathroom and returned with two glasses of water, handing one to Tooms. He nodded and Milton used the time to recall what Guthrie had told him. "Big advances. Those days they got only one or at most three eggs from a woman. Now…"

Tooms interrupted. "I'm pretty ignorant. How do they get the eggs? Cut 'em open?"

"No. The obstetrician sticks a needle through the belly wall into the ovary and with suction removes the egg from a follicle, you know a spot in the ovary, both ovaries, that develops each month and sends an egg or more down the tube to be fertilized."

"Yeah, and if not, the woman has a menstrual period."

Tooms beamed with pride at his knowledge of biology.

"Since then they have learned to give drugs, hormones, that make the woman produce more eggs, more follicles. And with better ultrasonography they may get as many as eight eggs at one time." He paused. Tooms seemed absorbed, so he continued, "They put an ultrasound probe in the woman's vagina and can very accurately know when the perfect time is to go after the eggs. Using the ultrasound, the doctor guides the long needle, now quite accurately, at a follicle and probably always gets an egg."

"Do they still need to implant so many eggs, chance getting multiple births?"

"Guthrie says the success rate is close to 50 percent nowadays, but some still put in many embryos. Irresponsible, as you know from reading about women that have four or five kids at once. I remember reading about a couple women who had six or seven. Dumb doctors. Many women probably have had that many grow but chose that heinous act, partial abortion."

"Fifty percent leaves room for improvement, doesn't it?" Tooms drained the glass.

"In normal conception one in four fertilized eggs implanted in the woman's uterus aborts." Milton grinned. "I doubt man will get much closer to God's success of 75 percent."

"Still, with so many eggs harvested, many spares are left for research, eh?" His voice changed, a taunting tone, and Tooms wiggled his eyebrows at Milton.

"Before the law changed and spares couldn't be used for research, the labs began to freeze eggs that weren't implanted initially. Some doctor in Paris developed a way to freeze the eggs and fertilize them if subsequently needed, if the first implants aborted. That was in 2002, but was stopped when the law changed eighteen months ago." Milton yawned, stood and kicked off his shoes. "I'm bushed."

Tooms grabbed his shoes and pushed out of the chair. "Thanks. That was good. Next time will you tell me what stem cells are, how they get them, and the business of genes?"

Milton eased over and patted Tooms's back. "Way beyond my knowledge. Ask Doctor Benz." He paused to consider whether to tell Tooms she also was a product of IVF. "She learned all that stuff as a med student."

Tooms left. Milton curled up on the small sofa in the church office, his head filled with bits and pieces of the recent dialogue and then many innuendoes from his conversations with Susan. *FBI seems to have things under control. Susan is another matter. Did she want to see me just to be my doctor? Will I see her and enjoy times like this afternoon?*

# FOUR

Susan Benz suffered through a tedious day at the Daniel Boone Clinic. With only minor injuries and common everyday illnesses she felt more like a first-aid worker than a doctor. So many patients came to the clinic that she had to work all day Thursday, normally her afternoon to be free. Frustration had mounted with each additional patient she saw, because for the past two days she had not been able to reach Milton and strangely he had not called. She had planned to see him, remove his stitches and the tape from his chest during her afternoon off work. For a brief moment she had even considered canceling her visit to the Curewell Clinic, but instead, she had delayed her visit to the end of the day.

She looked at the ape of a man sitting on the end of the exam table, struck by his attire, different from the usual dress of eastern Kentucky. His potbelly, rather than hanging over his belt, thrust it out. A wide black belt sported a large silver-looking buckle with a green cattle skull and horns attached. Susan watched as he pulled off the left boot. Also unusual, his boots were old, beat-up cowhide, their color difficult to discern because they were weather-worn with part gray-black and areas of deep brown that melted into brown-black sweat lines near the creases of the forefoot. While he pulled off his sock, she studied his face. Bushy eyebrows seemed to be a deeper brown than the generous mustache. He had a broad nose, its nostrils flaring when he told her he had a fungus under the nail of his big toe.

Susan sat on a metal stool, pulling it close to the end of the table. Sure enough she could see the inner third of the nail was thick and irregular, a faint yellowish color compared to the pink color of the rest of the nail.

"What about the other foot?" She cast a glance at the foot with the cowboy boot.

"None on the right one, Doc," he said in a drawl, typical Texas.

"Onychychronosis. Usual type. You say it bothers you? Getting tired of filing down the diseased part so it doesn't dig into the flesh?" She looked up from the foot and saw him nod the affirmative. "That's the easy way to keep it from troubling you—and inexpensive. Two options: I can have one of our surgeons remove the nail. Pretty painful, but quick. The other is medicine. Ten years ago you had to take an anti-fungal for one year to get rid of the fungus permanently. Latest drug takes only three months. It's very expensive. Does your health insurance pay for drugs?"

"Don't cover drugs, but I got money. No problem. I'm tired of the business—file and file some more and then pry up the nail and cut back the yellow part so it doesn't dig in, always with bleeding, a real pain in the butt—so could you write me a prescription, Doc?"

Susan watched the man as he spoke. His facial expression, his body language didn't match the discomfort he described. *He's the last add-on and over nothing but a nuisance,* she thought, searching the shifty eyes. *Weird eyes,* she told herself and concluded, *He looks mean, an angry demeanor, even when he puts on a half-smile.*

"Well, is that so difficult, Doc?"

Susan hated the way he said *doc*, a mocking tone to his voice. She pulled a prescription pad from her coat pocket and wrote the prescription. She narrowed her eyes as she tore it from the pad and handed it to him. He had replaced his sock and boot and stood when she gave him the prescription. Standing next to him jarred her memory bank. "You look familiar. Were you ever a patient at UK?"

With a sardonic smile he said, "We've seen each other couple times. Passed in the hall. I live upstairs in the same apartment building."

The eyes, the curling of his mouth, sinister almost, made a shiver creep up Susan's back. "Of course." She opened the exam room door for him. He left.

As she pulled out of the clinic parking lot, images of the cowboy's mean face generated a query, *Such a minor problem, and as an add-on he waited ninety minutes. I have a feeling he doesn't intend to fill the prescription.* Susan steered the Chrysler for Route 421. At the stoplight she removed her white coat and threw it on the back seat. At the corner she turned left onto 421. Passing the state police building, she recognized Tooms's car, a reminder of Milton's battle with her destination, Curewell Clinic, one mile north. *I must establish a contact, find out if they are behind the bombing attack on his house*, she resolved.

The Chrysler convertible eased past Walmart and Ace Hardware. She slowed when the former Do-It-Center, converted three years ago into the clinic, loomed on her left. Susan found an empty parking space to the left of the main entrance. After climbing out of the car, she snatched the white coat from the back seat and put it on. *A good calling card*, she decided. Curiosity had driven away her concern for Milton, and as she stepped into the reception area, her senses perked up.

"May I help you?" A middle-aged woman sat stiffly behind the reception counter, high enough to hide all but her head and neck. A plastic smile greeted Susan. After a quick glance around the room, Susan decided its appointments were out of place for the clientele it served in poverty-stricken Appalachia. Surely the oil paintings, most illuminated by ceiling well lights, meant little to these mountain people, she reasoned. A recollection hit her brain. *This is the area that demonstrators trashed three weeks ago. Maybe it wasn't so out of place before,* she decided.

Approaching the counter, she said, "I'm Doctor Benz—to see Marion Taswell."

The well-coiffured head lowered and after a brief period, a muted voice said, "I don't see you on her appointment list, Doctor. May I ask your business?"

Before Susan could respond, a door to the far right opened and a lithe figure in a white dress bounced across the room. The woman appeared to be around thirty. Her reddish-brown hair hung loosely to her shoulders.

A youthful exuberance matched her demeanor as she said, "Doctor Benz, I'm Marion Taswell." She smiled and said, "But of course you remember me...husband Joe's heart attack. So good of you to come this late in the day. I know you must be tired." She paused, and as if to confirm the lateness, stared at the wall clock that said 6:05. "I'll give you a quick tour today and later we can arrange a more comprehensive one."

Susan returned the smile, noting the receptionist's cold stare while she thumped her lips with the end of a pencil. "Yes, today seemed rather arduous. No big problems but just a bunch of pesky, unsatisfying ailments," Susan said and followed the young woman through the door.

Taswell showed her several examination rooms, typical rooms seen in any gynecologist's office. Each was well equipped, the furnishings upscale for the clientele, Susan reasoned.

"How long have you worked here, Marion?" she asked as they entered a larger room at the end of the hall. From its appearance, Susan knew it had to be an operating room.

Taswell stopped just inside the room and said, "Two years. I worked in Lexington at the University Hospital after I got my nursing degree." She beamed at Susan. "I met this wonderful man. He was one of my patients. We married and moved here. He works in the sawmill north of Baxter."

Susan said, "I went to UK med school and interned there."

"You look familiar. I believe you were assigned as a third-year student to my ward," Taswell said.

"Why, yes. General surgery, true to Kentucky's civil war posture, had a blue and a gray service. If I recollect correctly, Marion, you worked on gray service ward."

"Correct." Taswell threw an index finger around the room. "In this room and the one across the hall—it's just like this one—we do abortions and harvesting of eggs."

Taswell led Susan into the hallway and pointed to a door at the end of the hall. "The laboratories for in-vitro fertilization, and producing embryos, are located in there."

"Do you…" Susan had started her question when her ears picked up a muffled sound of a door closing behind her. She continued, "Do you ever implant any? Or are all the embryos used for research?"

Taswell's mouth stuck in the open position. Her eyes stared over Susan's shoulder. Her demeanor had changed from warm and relaxed to stiff and cold. Susan turned slightly and glanced over her shoulder, spying a tall man in a long white coat striding toward them. His bushy gray hair bounced with each step. He presented a professional face.

Extending his right hand he said, "Doctor Benz from the University of Kentucky Medical School." He took the hand Susan offered. "How nice of you to pay us a visit." He turned his eyes on Taswell, a cloud moving across his face. "Mrs. Taswell, I don't recall you told me we were having a visitor."

Susan felt the chill and watched Taswell squirm under the stern glare. Those severe features picked her memory, so she said, "Doctor Burgess, Doctor Cranston Burgess, I am honored to be here and see this avant-garde medical facility." Her memory had conjured a picture of Burgess from a recent issue of the American Medical Association Journal. His picture adorned the page that described his nomination as the most distinguished alumnus of the University of Kentucky Medical School. He was one of the pioneers in stem cell research and world-renowned for some of his research on molecular aspects of stem cell function, the current hot direction in the entire area of cloning and embryonic stem cell research.

Burgess rubbed his chin while he surveyed Benz. "What brings you to Harlan, Doctor Benz?"

"I just finished internship at UK, Sir, and am employed at the Daniel Boone Clinic," Susan answered, watching the curious countenance of the lanky man change to a frown.

"You have interest in research or are you spying for the media—maybe for that radical preacher—that kid from the hillbilly church in Baxter?" Burgess finished with a scowl.

Rattled by the frontal attack, Susan stammered, "N-neither. I wanted—well you see…" His blue-gray eyes twinkled in derision. This calmed Susan's nerves. She folded her arms over her chest and made her coolest professional smile. "I'm a product of in-vitro fertilization. One of the field's earliest triumphs." She smiled at Taswell.

"Congratulations. So you're an IVF kid. Last Sunday's evening news showed you at Heiter's church. So which is it? Media or Heiter? Maybe FBI—they're snooping around here. Working for them?" Sarcasm seeped from Burgess.

Susan pursed her lips, debating the response. She started for the door to the reception area. At the door she turned and said, "I happen to be Pastor Heiter's doctor, looking after his injuries from the blast that destroyed the parsonage, the hillbilly one. The FBI is trying to find the bomber, Doctor."

Burgess had a sardonic look. "His own doing. What we do here is quite legal and morally correct. We supply stem cells to researchers who will be able to offer cures for many ailments." He turned and, passing Taswell, said, "Show this naïve doctor to her car, Taswell." He disappeared through the door to the laboratory.

On the front walk Susan stopped and searched Taswell's face. "I hope I didn't get you in trouble. Heiter thinks once two DNAs join, the sperm enters the egg, a being exists. I don't. Your doctor is paranoid."

Susan turned for her car, but Taswell held her arm. "That was for your benefit. He knows I told him you were coming for a visit. Cranston was devious, attempting to draw you out." She let loose of Susan's arm.

"Paranoia doesn't become a man of his reputation, Marion," Susan retorted.

"Not paranoia. Too many demonstrations and the last with damage to the clinic—all because of Reverend Heiter." Taswell headed for the front door, but stopped to face Susan. "Nope, Susan. He has a right to be concerned. He worked as a young gynecologist in Atlanta ten years ago when anti-abortionists bombed the clinic where he worked. His nurse was killed."

"So you think he is incapable of violence. He couldn't be behind the bombing of Heiter's house," Susan said.

"I didn't say that," Taswell said and disappeared into the clinic.

Susan went to her car and with the key in the door, paused to look over the roof of the car. The sun was disappearing behind the Cumberland Mountains. "I don't think Milton is safe—even with the FBI protection," she muttered.

Susan had driven to the south side of Harlan, nearing the out-skirts of town, before she realized a car followed. She pulled into the parking lot and parked in front of her apartment, but waited until the car pulled into the spot next to her. Her alert mode changed when she saw Tooms climb out of the Chevy and approach. She opened the door and stood.

"You followed me," she said.

Tooms smiled. "You need to be more observant. I was parked at the far side of the Curewell Clinic parking lot." He stopped two feet away and smiled. "With the violence that has hit this area and your association with Heiter, you need to be more alert, Doctor."

"How many people must I tell I'm only his doctor?"

"Come on, I want to buy you dinner," Tooms said.

Susan scrutinized the figure and was disarmed by the warmth it exuded. "I don't let older men take me to dinner, Tooms."

"Business, Doctor Benz. I'm happily married and old enough to be your father. We need to exchange information."

"Fine. There's a new restaurant a couple blocks from here." She pointed south, to her right.

Tooms headed for the driver's side of his car. "I'll drive."

Susan threw her white coat on the front seat of the Chrysler, locked the doors with the keypad and climbed in the front seat of the FBI auto. Tooms guided the car onto Route 421 and headed south. Two blocks away Susan pointed to a small white structure. Several cars were parked in front. A sign above the door said, Mountain View Café.

Holding the café door open, Tooms threw a finger toward a trailer parked across the road. "Have you noticed that?"

Susan looked over her shoulder and as she passed by him said, "Of course. I eat here often. It appeared about a week ago. Sometimes there's a car or two. Once a truck. Another time a van." At an empty booth she grinned at Tooms. "See, I am observant."

They sat and Tooms looked around. He had selected an isolated spot, the nearest person two tables away. He removed two beige sheets of paper from behind the catsup bottle and thrust one at Susan. While they studied the menus, he leaned over the table and said in a low voice, "FBI support trailer, Susan." He straightened, appearing worried.

Susan interpreted the look to be from the use of her first name. She smiled and said, "Good cover. I thought it was a construction company vehicle. Looks like it."

"A command center." Tooms half stood in the booth, leaning toward the window. He pointed. "That pickup with the phony company name is ours." He sat on the hard seat.

"Do some of your staff live in my apartment building?"

Susan's question seemed to grab Tooms's attention.

He glanced out the window, then studied her face. "No. Why do you ask?"

"All afternoon, supposedly my afternoon off, I saw add-ons. Maybe you know them as walk-ins, patients who don't have an appointment and think their problem can't wait." She paused when a frown grew on Tooms's face. "My point, the last patient was some weirdo. His problem was not an emergency, not even urgent. A nail fungus on a big toe, probably there for years."

"Doesn't sound like one of our guys," Tooms said.

"Good cover if he were—but the guy said he lives in my apartment. His demeanor was bizarre," Susan said.

Tooms smiled and said, "Good, you must stay observant. Our team thinks Curewell has shipped in a bunch of private security types. I wanted to discuss two items. First, tell me what you learned at Curewell?"

"Too elegantly appointed for their poor patients, or should I say their paid clientele?"

Tooms cast a bewildered look at her. "Clientele?"

"Well, they pay these poor mountain women to get their bellies punctured to harvest eggs. They aren't patients—those that get complications can be called patients."

"Their report to Washington said that they don't have any complications. Did you find out their complication rate? Tell me what you learned," Tooms said.

"Didn't get that far because the boss, Doctor Burgess, popped up and acted upset that I was getting a tour. Did you know he worked at the Atlanta abortion clinic that was bombed years ago? A young doc then. His nurse was one of those killed," Susan said.

"Yes. We have his life's story. One reason we are here to check on Curewell. He's been known to bend the law. We didn't believe his report of zero complications. And surreptitiously, we heard that he's doing late-term abortions. Remember when President Campbell signed the bill allowing the production of embryos for stem cell research, he limited non-therapeutic abortions to the first twelve weeks of pregnancy," Tooms said. He paused while Susan ordered a sandwich and coffee. He ordered a bratwurst and iced tea. "Are you going back? Or better, could you ask your friend to get some data—such as the number of abortions, the number of eggs they harvest, and complications of their procedures?"

Susan mulled over the request and said, "Doubt Burgess will let me visit again. He's terribly paranoid." She paused to swallow a bite of sandwich and after some cogitation added, "Taswell is a patient-friend, a grateful patient. She thinks I saved her husband's life. He had pain shooting up his neck to the jaw. I determined the pain was angina."

"Weird type pain from the heart. No?"

"Yes. Atypical referred pain from cardiac ischemia, Max. And the guy's young. Early forties," Susan said.

"Can you get data? And maybe if they do any late-term abortions?"

"I'll try to get some numbers about complications. Something Taswell said as we parted, but before she entered the clinic, makes me optimistic. As far as late-term abortions, that may be difficult, risky for Taswell. Since they know late-terms are illegal they either have two records or they falsify the original."

Tooms gulped some tea and said, "Tell me what Taswell said."

Susan hesitated while they ordered dessert, a scoop of chocolate ice cream for her, apple pie à la mode for him. When she saw that the waitress was out of earshot, she said, "I asked Taswell if Burgess was incapable of violence, the attack on Milton's house. She retorted, 'I didn't say that.' She's bringing her daughter in for a checkup next week. I'll give her a laundry list."

Tooms smiled, nodding his approval. "The second thing. Heiter's not making Hank's job easy. Two days ago he slipped out of town to Richmond to a conference. Didn't tell Hank. Abel's a compulsive nut. He threatened everybody he could find to tell him where Heiter went. I'm surprised he didn't quiz you."

"He did. Asked me if I knew where Heiter went. I didn't know he had left town. He should have told me." Susan looked up from her ice cream and, noting the peevish look on Toom's face, she added, "He needs his stitches out and the tape off his chest."

Tooms grinned and said, "Of yeah, the second business was about stem cells. The last time I talked with Heiter, he told me lots about in-vitro fertilization—technique, results, and improvements. When I asked him to tell me about the production and details of using stem cells, he pleaded ignorance and told me to ask you."

"Here's a primer for you, simple basics, Max," Susan said and searched her brain for a spot to begin. "When an egg is fertilized by a sperm, a single cell is created. It has the potential to form an entire organism. The egg is totipotent. During the first hours the egg divides into two cells, each having the potential, if placed in a woman's uterus, of developing into a fetus. About four days after fertilization and several cycles of cell division, these totipotent cells begin to specialize, forming a hollow sphere of cells. Inside the hollow sphere is a cluster of cells called the inner cell mass." Susan searched Tooms's face. He seemed to understand so she continued, "The outer cell layer forms the placenta and supporting tissues needed by the fetus in the uterus. The inner cell mass forms all the fetal tissue. The cells are called pluripotent. At five days after fertilization the inner cell mass begins to separate, shows signs of cell differentiation. This is the time selected by many in-vitro fertilization clinics to transfer the embryo from the petri dish to the uterus. Also at this time embryo stem cells are derived, probably 200 to 250 cells."

Tooms waved a hand at Susan. He summarized what she had told him and asked, "Is that pretty close—how it goes?"

"Not bad for a supercop," Susan said. "The reason researchers use embryonic stem cells rather than adult stem cells—adults do have some, you know—is that they are difficult to get and not all are predictable how they differentiate."

"That why, after Bush banned production of embryonic stem cells for research, our guys had a flurry of investigations?" Tooms smiled and offered more, "We caught a few labs covertly making embryos for research, until President Campbell made it legal. Still, we must monitor them for compliance, complication rate, and to make sure they aren't in violation of law."

"You mean cloning of humans, not just to make a person, but for research," Susan said. Recalling the skirmish about cloning, she added. "I remember when a private lab, maybe that was eight years ago, reported they had employed the same technique used to clone sheep—remember Dolly—to clone a human embryo. They claimed only for research purposes. The ensuing outrage whipped the U.S. Senate into action. They had refused to pass the House bill that made it a crime for researchers to use embryos for stem cell research."

"Very good, Susan," Tooms said. "President Bush called cloning immoral. That heaped a lot of pressure on the senators. And so in '03 the law stated that use of embryonic stem cells and the cloning of human embryos for research was a crime. Before that legislation, those with government grants could not use human embryo stem cells for research. Bush tried to dissuade privately funded research and made cloning of humans illegal."

Susan's brain pulled up an image of Heiter's fierce expressions during his sermon. She said, "President Campbell changed all that. Milton must have had a fit when Congress passed a law making legal the cloning of human embryos and use of stem cells for research. That started the demonstrations and protests similar to those against abortion in the nineties."

Tooms waved a finger at Susan. "Campbell and many politicians thought that banning cloning to make a human being would quell the anger. They should have made cloning by off-shore labs a crime."

"I can't believe that goes on, what with the weird forms cloned by the off-shore labs. They produced some pathetic organisms."

Tooms gasped, "Try monsters. Stumps for legs, tiny heads, heavy bodies—same as the forms from that chemical technique called pathogenesis."

Susan smiled and said, "Close, supercop, pathogenesis fits the product." She hesitated to let Tooms speak. He just stared so she continued, "The word is parthenogenesis, the production of an individual plant without fertilization. Biologists have known about the process for years. At the turn of the century researchers found a chemical that would induce a human embryo to undergo division without fertilization—by parthenogenesis."

"Wow! That was exciting in the scientific world," Tooms said.

"Actually, scientists had known for years that the process occurred in some animals, stimulated by mechanical or chemical means," Susan told Tooms. For a moment she considered the drift of their dialogue. "The point of all this is to say that I'm not against embryo stem cell research or cloning of human embryos for research. I don't see the distinction—why that should have prompted moral indignation and passage of the law—any more than embryonic stem cell research, because neither are beings."

"Heiter know that's what you believe?" Tooms scooted over and stood, helping Susan stand.

As they walked for the door Susan replied, "He does. We argue over when a fetus or an embryo is a being. Yet, probably because I'm a doctor, I am more worried about all the frozen sperm, eggs, and embryos that parents and relatives fight over. You want to get into a legal and ethical quagmire? Just think of all the mind-boggling issues concerning the rights of parents, surrogates, kin, and others. I'll give you a couple examples. First, husband doesn't want any more kids but his wife does and thus asks to be impregnated. Whose right is upheld? What if they are divorced or the husband is dead, or his kin want to place an embryo in a surrogate? A second case would be just to reverse their roles and have the wife deceased, and her family does not want her egg or their embryo to be put into a surrogate so the father, an ex-convict, can't have their child. That's only the tip of the iceberg. There are so many technical, legal, and ethical problems involved in genetic engineering and harvesting of embryos."

"Wow! Stop. I can't take all that in. I thought this was merely a simple protest march by a bunch of fundies trying to stop scientific and humanitarian advances. Thank goodness we're here."

Tooms dropped Susan at her apartment. She tried to reimburse him for her part of the check, but he refused, telling her it was a business expense.

Unable to reach Milton by phone again, Susan went to bed with a resolve, *I must see him and remove his stitches.*

Yet she felt some relief that she didn't have to look into those searching eyes.

# Chapter
# FIVE

**Shrill** ringing invaded Milton Heiter's mental voyage into the realm of the numinous. He continued to press on the last tile he had crafted for the bathroom floor, turned his head toward the door and yelled, "Jethroe, come here." When the gangly man stood over him, Milton said, "Kneel down here and put pressure on this piece of tile while I answer the phone."

As soon as the boy applied pressure with a hand, his closeness sending a waft of strong body odor, Milton dashed for the phone in the living room. He snatched the black receiver from its cradle. "This is Pastor Heiter."

"About time you came home. Want the stitches to grow into your brain?"

Milton smiled when he recognized Susan's voice. "Well, you never call, never came to see me. You are neglecting your patient, Doctor."

"Pooh. I've tried to reach you, but you slipped out of town, escaped your guard, Hank," Susan said.

"He certainly perseveres. He found me in Richmond. I thought that pretty stupid until he told me some guy was shadowing me," Heiter said. He changed the phone to the other hand. "That's ridiculous—someone way up in Richmond. I think he probably wanted an excuse to get near Washington, probably see a girlfriend on government time, our taxpayers' dollars."

"Quit stalling. When can I take out your stitches, Milton?"

"Doctor Benz, you can take them out now. In fact, put on work clothes, and after you play doctor, you can help. I just put down the last tile in the bathroom. Any good with a brush? Jethroe is painting the bedroom, and I was about to tackle the living room," Milton said.

"I'm on my way," Susan said and hung up.

Milton noted the time, nine-thirty. She must not have clinic hours on Saturday, he decided, and went to see how Jethroe was doing. He found the young man as he had left him.

"You can ease up, Jethroe. It's stuck well enough," Milton said. He looked around the room. "Doctor Benz is coming to help me paint the living room. See if you can find another brush, Jethroe." Milton patted Jethroe's shoulder. "Doing a neat job in the bedroom. It looks good."

After cleaning the excess grout from the light brown tiles on the bathroom floor, Milton went into the bedroom, where Jethroe was busy painting the far wall. He organized a bucket of pale blue paint, took the brush Jethroe handed him and went to the living room. As he placed drop cloths along the wall near the front door, he heard a car door shut. He opened the door and watched Susan take the porch steps two at a time. A stained white T-shirt hung almost to mid-thigh. The old tennis shoes had a variety of paint spots. A blue faded baseball cap partially covered her hair.

"Do I look so shabby?"

Milton realized he was staring intently. He cast a sheepish grin. "No, it's just I haven't seen you in casual...work clothes."

"Should I have worn something else?" Susan walked past him and surveyed the room.

He started to shut the front door but stopped when Susan wrinkled her nose and said, "Whew! Body odor. And it's heating up out there."

Milton took the hint. He shoved the door against a wall and propped it open with a chair. "Well, for this environment bib overalls would be perfect, but you look fine," Milton said, watching her scrutinize the large floor-model television set. "You get to swat any mosquitoes or flies that join our work party."

"For someone who doesn't watch television you certainly have a large, expensive set," Susan said and glanced sideways at him. "Does Hank always sleep on the couch?"

He stepped to the hall doorway and peered toward the bedroom. With Jethroe working out of earshot, he moved next to Susan and in a low voice said, "Hank is compulsive. Nobody would ever know he sleeps here. The TV? FBI setup, one of their surveillance pieces. It…"

Susan interrupted him. "You mean it's not a TV?"

"Oh, it's a TV," Milton said and went over and turned it on. The travel channel displayed pictures of the Suez Canal. "And more, Doctor. Before I left, some workmen put a special antenna on the roof. It has eyes, infrared and daylight, directed by motion detectors. All that so they can watch the perimeter of the church property. Fancy setup. In addition to visual surveillance and motion detectors, they have installed audio recorders. The pictures are digital, stored in a computer in the church office along with any sounds captured."

"Clever, I saw the new antenna on the roof. I didn't notice any on the church. How does the computer get input?"

Milton walked to a window facing the church and pointed toward the roof. "See the lightning rods? Well, they are special antennae for sending and receiving signals."

"Send? To where?" Susan stretched her neck to stare at the lightning rods.

"Abel isn't the most talkative guy, but I got it out of Max. They have a communication trailer south of town. People sit there and can hear or see everything along the property perimeter. And Abel can flip a button on the back of that," Milton turned and pointed at the TV, "and at night or any time see what the roof antenna captures or listen to outside sounds."

"So at night the crew in the trailer awakens him. And he can see what goes on from the couch where he sleeps." Susan surveyed a deep blue piece of furniture.

"Pull-out, called a futon. Yeah, he doesn't miss any sleep unless something suspicious occurs," Milton said.

"You need it. I visited Curewell Thursday and I think they are capable of anything to protect their enterprise," Susan said.

"I feel safe. In fact, it seems a bit overdone," Milton said. He walked over and picked up a brush, handed it to Susan and continued, "Remember that wristwatch Max talked into last week?" When Susan nodded her head, he added, "Well, Abel has a slightly larger version. That computer in my office can transmit sounds and pictures to him anywhere. Satellite—I mean literally anywhere."

Susan grabbed the brush and said, "I heard that technology was developed for the war against terrorists."

In two hours they had covered the two unpainted walls in the living room. Both washed paint spots from their hands and faces in the kitchen sink and cleaned the brushes. With the drop cloths stored on the back porch, they replaced the furniture and stood admiring their work.

"What do I get paid? It looks nice. Abel should have pleasant dreams," Susan said.

"I doubt he is capable of pleasant dreams, Doctor," Milton said and paused to study Susan, then added, "For pay, I thought a picnic at my favorite mountain retreat would be appropriate."

He opened the refrigerator, surveying the contents, suddenly aware of Susan's warmth as she leaned over his shoulder and peered into the refrigerator.

She straightened and said, "Lotsa choices. How about ham and cheese sandwiches?"

Milton nodded yes, so she directed him to get the bread and a sack. While she made the sandwiches, he retrieved two apples from the vegetable bin on the porch and threw them into the bag.

"Have any cold drinks, Milton?"

"Doctor, I have some in the Pepsi machine in the church office. Come," Milton said.

Susan frowned and followed. Crossing the yard to the chapel she told him she needed to go to her car and fetch her medical bag so she could remove his stitches. Milton entered the church office and put coins in the Pepsi machine. He put two cans of pop in the lunch bag and turned when Susan entered, bag in hand. She placed the black bag on the desk and told Milton to remove his shirt.

At her instructions he sat on the desk and stared as she studied the tape. After she freed up the ends of the four strips, she told him to take a deep breath. With one mighty yank she peeled the tape from the right side of his chest.

"Ouch, Doctor. You took half my skin," Milton yelled, but with a smile. He felt a strange sensation as she squinted and gently rubbed a hand over his chest.

"Poor baby," she cooed, looked in his eyes and said, "Removing the stitches from your head will hurt worse if you persist in calling me doctor, Milton. Now turn around."

Her face was cold but he detected a twinkle in her eyes. He climbed off the desk, sat in the chair, folded his arms on the desk and buried his face in them. "This okay, Susan Doctor?"

"Just fine, Milton Reverend." He felt a stitch pull and then another, and another, until he had counted twelve. She pulled up his head. A curious look covered her face.

"Susan," he said. He paused, stood and gazed deep into her eyes. "Thanks for being my friend. I don't want to be impertinent, but I do like you a lot for knowing you such a short time."

Susan put the instruments in her bag and said, "Calling a woman by her first name isn't impertinent or intimate, Milton. If you're my friend, it's quite proper, even for a preacher."

Milton grabbed the lunch bag and Susan her medical bag. They went to her car. She put down the convertible top and placed the black bag and lunch sack in the back seat. After they traveled two blocks on Route 119, Milton directed her to turn left onto Route 421 toward the Cumberland Mountains.

"Where does this go?" Susan asked, glancing in his direction.

The movement with the wind in the open vehicle made her appear fresh, happy. Without the baseball cap the wind whipped her hair to and fro. The sloppy paint shirt gave her a young girl appearance. The scene eased his tired feeling and his worries of the past weeks. He half-turned in the seat and said, "To Mozelle, but we will take a left on 221 about six miles up the mountain. A little way on it and we'll go right on an unmarked road that leads to a secluded spot." While Susan kept her eyes glued to the curving mountain road, she asked him where the FBI fancy computer in his office was hidden.

"In the Pepsi machine," Milton answered and when she shook her head disbelievingly, he told her, "Abel came in dressed in a Pepsi driver's uniform and told me he was donating a pop machine for my office. I hung around and watched. The back of the machine has a compartment that holds the computer. Clever, how he hid the wires to the lightning rods." Twice Milton had glanced in the side view mirror and noted cars some distance behind.

After traveling fifteen minutes, they eased onto a gravel side road from 221. He stared at the mirror; one car zoomed past the exit, but a black one slowly turned onto their road. Susan turned the car where he pointed along a grassy road with only two tire tracks to guide the way. *Black car, FBI, Abel is playing protector*, he concluded. A quarter mile farther and Milton motioned for Susan to stop. They climbed out and he grabbed the lunch sack and blanket. He led her around a stand of saplings to a huge oak tree. She stopped and pointed to a small meadow to their left and then a brook ten feet to their right. He helped Susan spread the blanket beneath the tree, one edge within a foot of the stream bank.

While she spread the lunch on the blanket he told her that many times he had seen whitetail deer in the meadow. Both ate in silence, Milton certain Susan was mesmerized by the babbling brook. Now and then the shrill call of an osprey or the jabbering of a jay pierced the rhythmic sound. He started to speak but was halted by a faint breeze that whispered through a stand of nearby willows.

Susan put down half of her sandwich, reached behind her and produced a palm-sized cellular phone. Milton watched as she dialed.

She spoke into the phone. "Yes, operator, I was just checking to see if this gadget worked up here." She paused, mouth open and then said, "I know it's satellite, but I had heard there can be blind reception spots up here in the mountains." Susan paused again, glanced at Milton with a faint smile. "No, I'm not on call, but if you get any long-distance calls for me, please call my cellular number." She stuck the phone in a hip pocket.

"Long distance. Any problems?" he asked.

Susan looked from the brook. "Not really. My father frequently calls me Saturday afternoon." Glancing around, she said, "You know, it's too bad we professionals don't take once a week and enjoy the peace and quiet of nature."

Milton liked that. He lay back propped on an elbow and watched, enjoying the wiggle of her nose when she spoke. He said, "Remember when the terrorists flew our planes into the World Trade Center? I was in college. That took the heat off my drive as a college student, pre-theology, to prevent the use of embryos for research. The light shone on terrorists: Afghanistan, Iraq, and Somalia, their safe havens. And I..." He stopped and stared to his right. He squinted and raised to a sitting position.

"See a deer?" Susan looked in the direction of the meadow.

Milton's eyes searched the far edge of the meadow. "I saw a man, looked like a hunter in the maples on the far side." He chuckled. "Bet it's Abel, one of his creative covers. I spotted his car following us here."

Susan said, "I don't see anybody." She turned to Milton. "During that infamous terrorist attack, I was in high school. Not much impact on my life. But when they spread radiation with an ordinary bomb two years later, that somehow hit home."

"And within a year of that they sabotaged Argonne. That killed my pa." He paused when a picture of his father surfaced in his mind. "It took a few years for me to consider embryo stem cell research anything more than some obtuse, almost irrelevant problem."

"Seems a long time ago. They caught most of the terrorists. Destroyed Al Qaeda and only now and then some threat appears," Susan said.

"And I wonder how many of those are from some sicko, copy-cat terrorist, born here in the U.S.?"

"You mean like the guy who blew up the federal building in Oklahoma City at the end of the last century?"

"Yeah," Milton said. He watched Susan pucker up one side of her face. She took a bite of sandwich. "Do you think God sends bad things to our country, a Christian country?"

A chuckle escaped from Milton. He faced her, distracted momentarily by what he read in her eyes, a captivating look. "You may not recall, but after the terrorists hit the World Trade Center and the Pentagon, the media sprang their usual trap to discredit Christian leaders."

"You mean like the atheist you told me about?" Susan asked.

"No. Two televangelists. Robertson and..." Milton hesitated, when a faint cough sounded from the willow on the opposite side of the brook. Susan followed his gaze.

The lower willow branches moved. He stiffened until a voice he instantly recognized as Abel's said, "Don't look over here. And do exactly as I say. We have company."

Susan looked at her lap, but Milton stared at the willow and said, "I saw you across the meadow a bit ago. A hunter isn't..."

Abel's soft tone turned harsh. "Doctor Benz. This preacher may not care if his head gets blown off, but my boss would be furious, so listen. Push the reverend to the ground. The two of you lay on your bellies. If he's too square, draw close and put your arm around him."

Before Milton could retort, Susan had crushed him onto the blanket and turned onto her stomach. He rolled over as Abel's directions played in his brain. Milton wiggled close and put an arm around Susan's waist. She giggled, their faces inches apart. He raised his head and looked over his shoulder at the willow.

"Okay. Any other orders? What's up?" Milton hissed.

"Keep your heads down, both of you. I've been on this side since you arrived. Company on the other side of the meadow has a rifle, not a squirrel rifle. I've called for backup. Go ahead and continue your weird discussion, but keep your heads down and you'll be fine."

Milton rested his head on the blanket and searched Susan's eyes. She stared at him and said, "I, too, saw Abel's car in the rearview mirror. And another car. It didn't turn when we got on the gravel road." She smiled, a peevish one. "Now what were we discussing?"

Milton's face felt warm. Susan's presence, her warm body under his arm, brought out long quiescent feelings. "I believe I was talking about televangelists. I still forget the other. But they said in so many words that God sent that tragedy to the U.S. because of our sins, such as abortion, use of embryos for research, illegitimate births, divorce rate, acceptance of gays and lesbians and other evils in the country."

"And you probably agreed with them," Susan said.

"I did. But under the heat, Robertson and his colleague apologized. I'm sure they believed in their heart what they said."

Susan tilted her head, looking toward the green canopy and said, "So why did they recant?"

"Those were the days of political correctness, even Christian political correctness. You didn't ever say in public what you strongly believed if it might offend someone," Milton said.

"So you believe your loving God punished his people with terrorists' attacks just like all those stories in the Old Testament?" Susan moved her head closer and squinted at him.

"No, not that way. He…" Her warm breath hit his face, her scent engulfed him.

Susan beamed, "You're hedging. Did God send punishment or not, Milton?"

He studied her face. "Like Jesus, who said he came not to bring peace but send a sword, God sends troubles when we break his commandments," Milton said.

"So, you're saying He does."

"That's simplistic, the way the media try to trap Christians, Susan. It's this way; when we break God's laws, trouble comes. God's laws aren't some irrational tenets to please Him. They are psychologically powerful guidelines for His sheep, and when we follow them we live with inner peace and outer peace. Mind you, our actions offend non-believers who sometimes resort to evil, as happened with the terrorist attacks."

"I still don't get it," Susan said.

"Okay. Let's start with the Lord's commandment, 'Thou shalt not kill.' Our country was founded by violence. During eight years of the revolution we didn't just kill British soldiers. We killed loyalists, Americans. And we acquired much of the southwest by war, killing, and we took lands from the Native Americans. The slavery issue—well, the breakup of the union—was settled by civil war, lots of killing. Violence and violent heroes were portrayed in books, and later in movies and television."

Susan grinned and said, "And we furnished arms to Israel in their fight with the Palestinians. We took their side, so you say the Islamic radicals paid us back."

"I already told you a mad dog has to be killed to prevent wasting of human life. I can't draw a neat line in complex worldly conflicts, but certainly, as I said before, Adolph Hitler, Saddam Hussein, Milosevic, Bin Laden and maybe for other terrorists who refuse to give up, killing them may be the only way to prevent further atrocities," Milton said. He searched his mind for a clearer way to show her how evil comes to sinners, not necessarily sent by God, but her closeness—the warmth—had turned to heat. Hesitantly he continued, "Capital punishment, sex out of wedlock, adultery, abortion, deviant sex—are all sins. Our violent society has been a manifestation of a stiff-necked people, defiant people who claim to be Christians, but don't act like Christians. Jesus asked a pertinent question in Luke 6:46. He said, 'Why callest thee me Lord, Lord, and do not those things I say?' God doesn't send troubles to us. We bring them on by not following his laws, the guidelines that would protect us. That's what the televangelists meant."

Susan pursed her lips. "So as a country we accepted, maybe legitimatized, sin, abortion, gays, lesbians, adultery and all that, along with the recent business of stem cell research and cloning. If I understand your reasoning, you believe that a country that grew by killing—even capital punishment—soon let political correctness change the norms of Christian behavior in the ole U. S., and in the absence of God's way, we reap the suffering those things generate."

"That's good. One can't describe in a sentence..." Milton's mind quit working. Susan's eyes had frozen his next thought. He took the arm from around her waist and rubbed her lips with his index finger. "You are special, Susan. When I'm with you, I feel..."

"You lovebirds can get up now." Tooms, dressed in a polo shirt and shorts, appeared from behind the oak tree.

Milton jumped up, pulling Susan after him. He surveyed the unprofessional garb of his FBI friend. "So what did you find over there?" He threw an arm at the far side of the meadow.

While Susan folded the blanket and gathered the empty cans and stuffed them in the sack, Tooms told them he and two other agents along with Abel found no one. He explained that they did find fresh boot tracks where a man, probably heavy, had hidden so he had a view of the oak tree and the two picnickers underneath.

The impact of the story hit Susan. She grabbed Milton's hand, squeezed hard. Their eyes met. They appeared to oscillate. Impulsively, Milton bent down and kissed her gently on the cheek, whispering in her ear, "It's okay. God just put us together. Nothing will happen."

Tears filled her eyes. She smiled and turned for the clump of trees where her car was parked, pulling him by the hand.

Tooms sprang in their way. "No. I'll take you back to the city in my car. They found tracks, same boot tracks around your car. The team is checking it over. A tow is on the way. We'll give it a good going over, lift any prints—check for a bomb."

"No!" Milton gasped and drew Susan close when he detected a tremor in the hand he held.

"Come," Tooms said and led them over the stream to his car parked on the gravel road.

Morbid silence fell on the two in the back seat of the FBI car. They held hands while Tooms told them of his concern for Milton and his worry that Susan could be collateral damage.

Upon arriving in the church parking lot, Tooms dropped off Milton, telling him to stay in the house until Abel arrived.

"I want to take Doctor Benz to her apartment, check it out and her neighbors. We'll set up some security measures for her, Milton, so you can go about your business."

Milton looked at Susan and muttered goodbye. He had only half turned for the parsonage when a body hit him. Susan clung to his neck. He felt her mouth at his ear. "In spite of this fright, I had a wonderful day. But I'm your friend. We're not lovebirds." She leaned back, her arms still encircling his neck. Emotions blocked his other senses. He saw tears in the corners of her eyes. *Her eyes didn't agree with her words,* he reasoned as he trudged for the parsonage. *They said, "I love you."*

The papers shook in his hands when Milton tried to review his sermon for the next day, so he put them on the kitchen table. He sank into a chair, laid his hand on the table and cried out to God, "Oh God, you promised you would never lay more on us than we could handle. Lord, it is one thing for me to be threatened and even give my life for you. But not Susan, Lord. Oh, my God! It's hard enough bearing the responsibility for the Caulders's deaths, but not Susan too, Lord. It's just too much to bear. So much innocent life lost. Oh, the thought of it! Please, Lord, don't let it happen. Put a hedge around Susan. Protect her, Lord. Put your armor on us, oh gracious Lord. Don't let it happen, especially now when I have finally found the love of my life, someone to share my spiritual pilgrimage. With her as my companion and you as Lord of my life, I will never have to be alone again. Hear my prayer, Lord, and bless your children everywhere."

Milton searched for more words to relieve the ache in his heart, but fatigue, physical and emotional, put a lock hold on his brain. He wept softly. Finally, Milton began to pray again, "Lord, guide the FBI in their investigation. Let them catch the killer and keep him from killing anybody else. Please, Lord, I implore you. Stop the violence. Bring this whole mess to a close. Yes, even the clinic and those responsible for the killing of the unborn. Oh God, give me wisdom and a discerning spirit to..."

A car door slammed, pulling Milton out of his trance-like state. Abel burst through the front door dressed in white coveralls of a tow truck operator. The sight struck a funny chord. "You look the best I've seen yet, Hank."

Abel's stern countenance didn't change. He pulled up a chair at the kitchen table and motioned for Milton to sit. He loosened the top buttons of the uniform and cleared his throat.

"Do any of your flock wear cowboy boots?"

Milton chuckled, "Hey, these are mountain folk. Never. Why? Is Susan safe, Hank?"

"The stalker across the meadow and the tracks by Benz's car were cowboy boots. A good lead. The boys are putting an alarm system in Susan's apartment and in her car. When it is set and somebody touches her car, the car blares at the world."

"So she's at risk because of me?"

"If the stalker is only half blind he can see that you two are in love. He would…"

Milton waved a hand in Abel's face and said, "Love, says who?"

Abel shrugged his shoulders. "Says? Nobody needs to say it. And if you can't realize it, you are in for a big fall. If he sees that you two care so much for each other, he can more readily get to you through Susan. She's at big risk, Reverend."

Milton folded his hands on the table, pretended to study them while he digested Abel's remarks. He scrunched up the left side of his face and looked into the penetrating eyes of Abel. "I've been so busy counseling her for her problems, I suppressed my deeper feelings, Abel. Tell me the significance of cowboy boots."

"Has anyone told you about the Brown boys?"

"Who?"

"Mort and Ezrah, the guys who were paid to blow up your old parsonage. When I quizzed them, they said they never saw the contact's face, only from the waist down. He wore beat-up cowboy boots and wore a cowboy belt," Abel said. He stood and began to remove the tow operator's uniform. He tucked his brown short-sleeve shirt in his pants and sat again.

"What kind of cowboy belt?"

Abel beamed, "Special one, a wide black belt with a large silver buckle. A green skeleton of a cow head and horns adorned the buckle."

Milton shook his head from side to side and said, "Nope. Never saw any parishioners—never saw anybody in these parts with such a belt."

"Good," said Abel. "When we find a guy who wears old weather-beaten cowboy boots and a distinctive cowboy belt, we've got our man. If we're lucky, we can tie him to Curewell and solve lots of problems."

While Milton listened, he went to a cabinet next to the sink, grabbed the aspirin bottle, and downed two white tables with a swallow of water. He saw Abel's quizzical look and said, "Must be all the excitement. I've been getting these headaches about evening time the past couple of days."

Abel stood and went to the doorway. He paused and said, "A little rest might help. I'll leave you to your Sunday preparations, Pastor."

Milton noted a faint smile and decided stone face had a warm spot after all. "Night, Hank," he said and sat down at the table. The sermon papers glared at him. "I must concentrate," he muttered. "I need help, Lord. This message must be clear—teach, and not anger, Lord," he prayed.

Chapter

# SIX

Sunday morning arrived with a cool breeze blowing south along the base of the Cumberland Mountains. Milton stood on the back stoop of the parsonage, weary from the eventful night. Eyes closed, he pointed his chin in the direction of the breeze and let it soothe his brow. He opened his eyes and watched the breeze blow the top leaves of trees at the back edge of the yard. They seemed to dance in the bright morning sunlight. "Ah Lord, you brighten my spirit. Help me this morning give your sheep sustenance for their soul, bright sunlight to let their spirit dance," he prayed out loud and walked toward the church, reviewing his approach to the service. True, he had changed his prepared sermon when he had reflected on the dialogue he and Susan had about the two televangelists. He had prayed for guidance, for a simple way to tell his flock that God doesn't use terrorists to punish his people; rather, they open the door to the devil by living sinful lives. Changing the message kept him up late, but the disturbance at three-fifteen in the morning was more responsible for his weariness.

The staff in the command trailer had awakened Abel because motion detectors had focused the roof cameras on a person prowling behind the parsonage near the spot where the trailer stood. Gun in hand, Abel apprehended the invader. The man's loud protestations awakened Milton. He recognized the voice making loud noises—Jethroe. As it turned out, Jethroe had left the old watch given to him by Milton on the back porch and out of guilt feelings he decided to retrieve it at that inauspicious moment. Milton convinced Abel that Jethroe was a trusted friend and meant no harm, so after a harsh scolding, Abel let Jethroe disappear into the woods behind the church property.

Lack of sleep hadn't helped his headache, so at the back door of the church, he paused to gulp down two aspirin. At five to eleven he knew many folks had been there for at least fifteen minutes, offering exhortative prayers. He reminded himself that not infrequently he was unable to participate in the session. Quietly, he entered the back door, eased to the altar railing and kneeled in prayer. The church was full, but not crowded with people standing along the sides or out in the parking lot as the previous week. He rose and went to the pulpit, put his papers on the lectern and surveyed the congregation. His eye spotted Susan two rows from the back. He liked that.

Milton's head began to throb, a distraction. He rubbed the spot above and slightly in front of his left ear while he waited for silence. The throbbing turned to a dull ache so he smiled, thanked them for their prayers and gave the invocation. "Yea, Oh Lord, though I walk through the valley of the shadow of death, I will fear no evil for Thou art with me, Thy rod and Thy staff they comfort me. Oh God, you are an ever-present help in every time of trouble. Wherever we go, Thou art there! On the highest mountain, or in the depths of the sea, Thou art there. To the farthest corners of the earth, desert or forest, Thou art there. Yea, whether it be New York City or Baxter, Thou art there. Yes, even in the presence of our enemies, Thou art there. Praise be to God, the living God—Emmanuel, God be with us. In Jesus name we pray. Amen"

Looking down at his notes, he grimaced, for the writing blurred. He shook his head ever so slightly, looked at those in the front rows. Their faces told him they noticed his odd behavior. He said, "Last week I was rather harsh, throwing you, me, and many Christians in the same basket, the one that holds our sins of omission. You know, those sins we commit because we are too lazy, cowardly or have other priorities. We know we should act responsibly, but we don't."

Some in the front row still frowned, and he sensed that others throughout the audience were distracted by his head shaking and head rubbing. "I apologize not for my pointed illustrations, but I do for my demeanor today." He rubbed the side of his head again to give them a hint. "Since last Sunday, events have unfolded in rapid succession, and I changed this morning's message in the wee hours of the morning. Please bear with me because I have wrestled with the delivery of the sermon so that it is crystal clear. You see, I would like to be less offensive because I angered some of you last week. My purpose is not to anger, but rather challenge." Milton looked at his notes, for the next cue so he could stay on track with his changed message. The words were still blurry. Panic. He slowly raised his head, afraid the long pause would make a restless congregation. Good, his mind flashed when he saw that they waited, expectantly.

He reached for his Bible, turned to the first bookmark and said, "The Old Testament lesson for today is from Joshua 24:15:

*Choose for yourselves this day whom you will serve, whether the gods of your forefathers served beyond the rivers, or the gods of the Amorites, in whose land you are living. But as for me and my household, we will serve the Lord."*

Briefly, Milton scanned the silent audience while his finger found the second bookmark. "The Gospel for today is Luke 20:25." He opened the Bible to the passage and read:

*"And he said unto them, Render therefore unto Caesar the things which be Caesar's, and unto God the things which be God's."*

He closed the Bible and while replacing it realized the words were clear, so he glanced at his notes. Clear. He smiled until his eyes made their way down the first page. He had skipped the opening hymn. Consternation made him grimace. Panic again. *Man, you have to concentrate, don't let weariness ruin your message,* he resolved. Still, when he looked at the congregation they didn't act like anything was wrong. *Well, some in the front pews have a curious expression,* he decided. He spied the Caulders in the third row on the left. Jethroe was seated next to his mother at the very end of the row. He looked alert, dressed in a white short-sleeve shirt, his hair combed back, shiny.

Milton produced his biggest smile and while looking at the Caulders, said, "Jethroe Caulder has helped me this week with painting the parsonage. A fine job he does. You'll see his handiwork when we have open house in three weeks. Last week," Milton paused while he fished in his left pocket for a coin. "I showed this quarter to Jethroe." He rolled the coin between his left forefinger and thumb, projecting his arm in front of the pulpit. "Whose image is that, Jethroe? Jethroe said, 'Pastor, that's George Washington, the first president of this country.' I smiled at Jethroe and told him to render unto Washington the things which be Washington's." A twitch of Milton's hand sent the coin rolling on the floor in front of the first row of pews. Ignoring the rattling sound it made in the perplexed silence and his fleeting concern at the uncontrolled twitching, he continued, sweeping his gaze from the Caulders around the congregation. He grinned at Jethroe and said, "That Jethroe is one smart lad. He said, 'That's like the Bible—the time Jesus told the chief priests and scribes when they questioned him that they should render to Caesar his things and to God the things that were his.' And so we, those of us who believe that a being exists as soon as a human egg is fertilized, whether in the uterus or in a petri dish, should render unto God the things which be God's. Beings are Gods. Psalm 24 says, 'The earth is the Lord's and the fullness thereof; the world, and they that dwell therein.' We Christians render unto Caesar the things that be Caesar's. We don't break Washington's laws. Neither does Curewell. They kill little beings, fetuses during abortions and embryos for stem cells, but they don't break Caesar's law. They are politically correct." Using his left hand Milton snatched the Bible from the shelf under the lectern and waved it vigorously. He scolded, "They don't render unto God, though, they break His law: Thou shalt not kill."

He replaced the Bible on the shelf and methodically searched the faces. "When we Christians demonstrate against the embryo factory this coming Saturday, we will not break Caesar's laws. Washington permits it. They grant us peaceful expression of our beliefs. We will not be politically correct, however, for we will render unto God the things that be God's next Saturday. We will be spiritually righteous. However, you Christians who remain politically correct and do nothing are not righteous and are sinning by omission for whatever be your motives. Like Joshua did, I call upon you. Choose for yourselves this day whom you will serve—join us and serve the Lord, and protect the defenseless."

Milton felt the excitement, the intensity in the audience. The adrenalin surge made his mouth dry. He reached with his right hand for the glass of water on the shelf next to the Bible. As he raised it to his lips, he used the interlude to glance at his notes for his next thrust. Blurry words brought out a frown. His right hand began to shake slightly and then more noticeably. Water missed his lips. Half the water ran down his front. Trembling, he attempted to replace the glass on the shelf. It missed and crashed to the floor. Milton knew from the noises emanating from the people that he needed to do something, anything to calm their reaction to his behavior. He blinked repeatedly, staring at his notes. Blurred words became double images, then one. His notes were clear. Thank you, Lord, he muttered and looked up. Susan approached down the center aisle. When she reached halfway to the front, Milton shoved his extended left arm, its palm aimed at Susan.

"Harlan's newest doctor has stood to be recognized." He hesitated because he wasn't certain if he should pursue the tack his mind had taken. "You all read what Mr. Zinger said about me. I am a product of in-vitro fertilization. A method for couples who have difficulty fulfilling God's commandment to procreate." Susan had stopped ten feet from the front so he asked with his eyes and mouthed, May I? To his surprise, Susan turned and faced the back.

She spoke, "I am a child of in-vitro fertilization as Reverend Heiter. Our parents render unto God. But I am also a product of a surrogate pregnancy, a medical advance that renders unto Caesar." She turned and smiled while she cast a quizzical look at Milton and approached the pulpit. Milton stretched both hands straight out over the lectern. No twitching. Softly he told her he was fine. Susan smiled and turned about. Finding a space in the first row of pews, she squeezed in between two buxom women.

"Thank you, Doctor Benz. That was a meaningful witness." He looked over the congregation and continued. "Surrogate pregnancy is a sin. Dr. Benz, the product, did not sin, but her parents and the surrogate sinned just as much as Abraham, Sarah, and her maid servant Hagar did when Sarah gave Hagar to Abraham to have a child. So we see that every medical advance is not spiritually righteous. For over three thousand years physicians followed the morals proclaimed by Hippocrates, called the father of western medicine. Their charge in treating patients was, 'do no harm.' When this Christian nation dropped atomic bombs on two Japanese cities in the great war of the last century—we lost almost 3,000 in the World Trade Center terrorism, Nagasaki lost 66,000 and Hiroshima 100,000—morals changed. The country accepted the moral from our atomic warfare. Better to kill close to a hundred thousand women and children than to lose several hundred thousand American and Japanese soldiers when the U. S. invaded the Japanese mainland. That was the guess, the prediction: the loss of hundreds of thousands if the bomb was not dropped. This then was easy for medicine to adopt, thus bioethics was born. And for over sixty years society has allowed the selection of the lesser of two evils and medicine has made the lesser of two harmful choices." Milton turned to the next pages of his notes. Blurry words stared at him. He blinked again, his peripheral vision noting that Susan scooted to the edge of her pew. He hurried on.

"Ten years ago our opponents justified the killing of embryos for stem cells by saying that research using them just might lead to a cure for cancer, might repair spinal cord injuries so paraplegics could walk, and on and on. For seven years they used stem cell lines, allowable by Washington law. And those who used stem cells from cord blood and adults made as many advances. Now after two years of making beings to be shipped around the world and killed to heal and cure, I ask you where are the cures? Is killing the littlest of beings the lesser of two evils? We must choose whom we will serve."

Milton still could not read his notes and his head began to throb again. "In conclusion, I want to ask where have our churches gone? They haven't gone anywhere and they still speak softly, politely, politically correct." He pounded the lectern as he thundered, "Political correctness has no place in God's realm, only in Caesar's. God's realm is spiritual righteousness and we Christians are called to be righteous before God. Choose this day whom you will serve."

He stepped from behind the pulpit. Weariness set in again. He wished he could gobble a handful of aspirin. "Please open your hymnals to page 110 and sing 'A Mighty fortress Is Our God.'" He read the faces, their shock that he did not line the hymn. They began to sing, "A mighty fortress is our God, a bulwark never failing; our helper he amidst the flood of ills prevailing." And so they sang forcefully. He beckoned to Susan. She came and while the congregation sang he told her he felt tired and this would be a good opportunity for him to show them that he trusted her moral medicine. She unobtrusively supported his left arm with one hand and held the hymnal for them with the other. The hymn ended with these words; "Let goods and kindred go, this mortal life also, the body they may kill; God's truth abideth still; His kingdom is forever. Amen."

Milton closed the hymnal, put it under the lectern and said, "This week you must render unto Washington the things which be

Washington's, but I also want you to be brave like Dietrich Bonhoeffer, the pastor Hitler hung because he remained spiritually righteous to the death. Bonhoeffer, unlike many German Christians, refused to be politically correct, to be a Nazi and participate in killing six million Jews. Hear what Bonhoeffer said, 'Christians are justified by faith through the grace of God given unto them through Jesus Christ. Good works, correct beliefs, belonging to a church, tithing and being baptized with water make us religious but do not make us ethical except maybe in the eyes of the world and our church.' Go forth this week and render unto Caesar those things that be Caesar's, but be spiritually righteous. Render unto God those things that be God's." Milton held Susan's hand with his right and raised his left. "Now go in peace. Serve the Lord. Amen."

Momentarily, he watched as the murmuring crowd departed out the front door. He knew this Sunday he was unable to dash out the back door to the front and shake hands. He led Susan into the office and retrieved two Pepsis. He handed one to Susan, who tilted her head to one side as she scrutinized his every move. He sat in the chair and waited for the medical interrogation.

Susan popped the can, took a sip, and in a metered voice said, "Care to tell me what was going on today?"

He gulped a mouthful of the cold, fizzy liquid, using it to wash down two aspirin. He pointed at the aspirin box. "Headaches. Right here." Milton pointed to a spot above and slightly in front of his left ear.

"Your gash, the blow to your head was back right. Correct?"

"Yeah, and last night's little sleep aggravated my headache. Must be stress. Some mighty strange goings on, Susan," he said.

They both sipped more Pepsi and she asked, "Any other symptoms? You didn't follow church routine, forgot the opening hymn, didn't line the closing hymn." She put the empty can on the desk. Her eyes grew. "And you dropped the quarter, spilled the water down your front and let the glass smash to the floor. Remember, we share, Reverend Milton." She finished with a smile.

To buy time for cogitation, he slowly finished off the Pepsi, placed the can next to hers and grinned. "No other problems," he lied and with a grin added, "Tired, weary from last night—this week, but our picnic spurred me through it all."

Susan squinted at him until he saw moisture on her cheeks. She climbed out of the chair, leaned over and pecked his chin. Two inches from his nose she said, "I worry so about you." She returned to the chair, wiped her cheeks with the back of a hand. Milton grabbed her hand before she could sit. They went to the parsonage to make sandwiches. Milton, moved by her concern, fell silent. Ringing from Susan's cellular stopped the reflective interlude. He watched as she put the small phone to her ear. Her eyes widened with a sparkle he didn't recognize.

"Dad! I was going to call when I got home this evening." Susan smiled at Milton, listening intently. "No. I'm not at work. I'm sitting in the kitchen of my favorite patient." She winked at Milton, shook her head. "Not a house call, either," she said with levity and continued, "and no, he's not sick."

Milton studied her body reaction that accompanied each response to conversation from her father. He went to the refrigerator, found lunch meat, cheese, and bread and put them on the table while listening. She stared at him, seeming absorbed. "That's easy." She gave Milton the once-over. "You told me you saw the news report on WGN TV after last week's media confrontation after church service. You didn't see me? I was there." While she listened, Milton asked in sign language what she wanted on her sandwich. She pointed to the bread and cheese so he made a cheese sandwich and put it on a salad plate before her.

As he filled two glasses with water, he heard her say, "Oh, he's better-looking than that. "I'd say six feet, not skinny but not an ounce of fat." She took a sip of water from the glass placed in front of her. A subtle frown appeared on her face. "Of course I told him I'm an IVF kid. So is he."

Milton sat and began to consume his lunch meat sandwich, washing a half-mouthful down with water when a scowl appeared on

Susan's face. "Of course, I like him—we're good friends. And no, we don't agree on a few science and religion issues." She started to nod her head and said, "Yeah, he thinks IVF is in God's plan." She wiggled her eyebrows at Milton. "But surrogate pregnancy is sinful. So is using embryos for research and…" Milton's mouth flew open. She squinted at Milton. When she took a bite of sandwich he figured she was on the receiving end of a long monologue.

She put the sandwich on the plate and changed the phone to her other hand. "Of course he knows. We don't have secrets—we share. And no, he's not a hillbilly." The smile during a brief pause told him the points were not serious. "He went to Garret Theological Seminary at Northwestern, knows of your reputation. Born outside Chicago, his father was a scientist at Argonne."

With the next pause she jumped out of the chair and walked around the table. Stopping across from Milton, she cast a blank look and said, "I told you we share—share everything. He knows about my sinful life, the affair, and the kid I got scrapped out." She sat and ate some sandwich, tilting her head as she chewed and listened. "Well, aren't we all sinners? After our dialogue about my wayward life, I feel just the way Jesus meant us to feel when we repent."

That statement stirred Milton's inner self. He threw her a kiss and smiled. She seemed to turn pink, looked at the cell phone. "He hasn't asked me yet. Doesn't matter. I said we are friends. I have no interest in marriage. I'm going to be the first female Professor and Head of Neurosurgery at a medical school. I haven't time for a family, and I certainly don't want kids that are raised by a nanny." She seemed to strangle the cell phone.

Milton shot a quizzical look at that exchange and cleaned off the table. Susan stood and said, "I will and no need to worry. I'm not in any danger and not much for him. Media are making news from a mole hill," she lied. She pushed the chair under the table and said goodbye.

Confusion bathed Milton's being. He stared at her as he said, "You have no interest in marriage—in a family. Certainly, you can't be serious. Maybe a ploy for a concerned father." He followed her as she headed for the front door.

Susan turned at the door and faced him. She smiled warmly when she said, "I like you lots. We are good friends. I can accomplish anything a man can, so I will be a Professor and Head of Neurosurgery just like my pa. Besides, if you and I, two professionals, married, the kids would be raised by a nanny." She continued to smile while she guided Milton to the futon. "You must rest." She departed.

Milton felt weary, anxious, and bewildered by the parting monologue. A nagging headache brought forth concerns. *I must rest so I don't get eyesight problems, get the shakes from being exhausted.* On the way to the bedroom, the next thought produced a frown. *So, she admitted to her father that having an abortion was sinful. Progress, Milt, old boy. And that comment she made that she isn't interested in marriage, in a family. What then?* That question propelled him into a deep sleep.

# SEVEN

The electric cautery in Susan's office sounded funny, a ringing instead of the grating buzz. She flipped all the switches, even turned off the machine. The ringing persisted until she realized she had been dreaming about removing cowboy's ingrown toenail with the cautery. She clapped her hands. The ringing stopped. Sitting on the edge of the bed, she peeked at the clock. It barked seven-o-one. Bright sunlight slanted through the small bedroom window. In the bathroom, a splash of cold water removed the last remnant of cobwebs. She brushed her teeth, staring at the mop head in the mirror. Susan removed the hairbrush from the cabinet behind the mirror and began to rid her Dutch-boy of its nighttime snarls. Strolling into the living room she felt the warmth of the early sunlight shining directly through the huge front window. At the window the brightness made her squint. She looked for her car until she realized that Tooms had dropped her off so that his crew could check it for fingerprints. He had told her that before the tow truck had removed it from the mountain meadow they had looked for and did not find a bomb.

After dressing and fixing her face for a busy day at the clinic, she went to the door to fetch the morning paper. Bent over, her hand hovered an inch from the paper resting on the hallway carpet. She sensed a presence before the words struck her ears.

"Not smart, Doctor."

Susan jerked upright, her eyes following from shoes to trousers to suit jacket to smiling face. "Don't you ever sleep, Max?"

"Never. I worry about you. What's the last thing I told you last night?" His smile faded.

Chagrin replaced Susan's brief fright. "Look through that before I open the door." She pointed to the convex eyepiece in her door. She leaned over and retrieved the paper.

Tooms said, "Remember, you may not get lucky with the next body waiting for you to get the daily rag. Had breakfast yet?"

"No. And I don't go to breakfast with older men, Agent Tooms," she said, jabbing his protuberant belly with the paper. "You ought to miss a breakfast now and then."

"Business, or did you forget you don't have a car. I'm your ride to the clinic," Tooms said.

"Guard my door. I'll deposit this inside and get my cell phone and bag—purse to you." Susan dropped the paper on the coffee table, paused long enough to open it and search the front page for Zinger's column. Not finding it, she went into the bedroom, put her cell phone into a brown leather bag she used for a purse.

In front of Mountain View Café, she turned and searched the vehicles parked by the FBI trailer. "Many cars and pickups, Max. Where's my poor lonesome convertible?"

On the way to a booth, Tooms told her it was a stone's throw away. He handed her a black object the size of her hand. "This is yours. Your car is behind the trailer getting fixed."

Susan held the light, thin object. Spying a lid, she opened it and saw a small opaque screen on one side, a bunch of buttons on the other. She looked up at Tooms and said, "A modern version of a palm pad."

Tooms leaned toward her, but turned his head when a waitress approached the booth. They both ordered, Susan toast and black coffee without sugar, and Tooms ordered bacon with one egg plus toast and coffee. The waitress left and he leaned closer. "That screen also has audio reception." He pointed to the side with rows of buttons. "The top three are for your car, the left one arms the security system, the middle unlocks the driver's door and the right one starts the car."

"Wow! I don't need a key. Why all the gadgets?"

"The security blasts the horn if someone breaks in, but that'll probably never happen. If a body gets within a foot of your car— when the system is armed—a voice barks a warning, and if someone, anything touches the car anywhere it'll send off a shrill siren. You understand the middle button. The..."

"Remote door opener is standard on many cars. But if one of my apartment neighbors parks next to my car, they'll most certainly send off the alarm," Susan said.

Tooms hesitated while the waitress put the food in front of them. "A lot happening today, Susan. At this moment, the crew is sweeping your apartment for bugs."

"Bugs?"

"Electronic listening devices. They will then install a security system, one that sounds an alarm and sends a signal to the trailer while turning on a surveillance eye in the hall. It will capture the culprit who tries your door," Tooms said.

"I can't believe all this is important, that someone would try to use me to get to Milton."

"Someone knew you were going to Heiter's Saturday." Tooms paused and pointed to the second row of buttons. "The left button turns off the system so you can enter your apartment. The middle one opens your door, which you will see has a huge electronically controlled bar on the inside—burglar proof lock." His finger hovered over the right button in the second row. "That red button is your lifeline. Any emergency, a threat, suspicious behavior by anyone who approaches, hit it. It activates the screen, so point it at the suspect—whatever—and talk. The audio system turns on, and both video and audio are instantly picked up by the crew in the trailer." Tooms leaned back and pushed his half-empty plate to the side. "Talk. Tell us what's happening, and if you can show us, point the screen."

"Hope I don't panic, hit the button needlessly."

"No such thing. If you think of using it, do it. Let me have your cellular." After she removed the cellular from her bag she handed it to him. "I'll give this back to you when you have no need for that. That new toy has your old cellular number." Tooms stuck it in his jacket pocket and pointed an index finger at the bottom row of buttons. "Those are just like on your cellular. So your palm pad is also your cellular phone. Except when you talk to us, hold it like this." He took the black object while Susan gulped a mouthful of coffee. He held it a foot from his face. "Make sure the screen catches your face while you talk and if you wish to capture someone or something in your area point the screen in that direction. It'll catch your voice easily."

Susan's mind whirled. While Tooms handed her the object and finished his coffee, she reviewed in her mind the function of each button. A smile erupted when she realized she had the security pad, video-audio pad, TV and cellular phone object mastered. *Fun*, she thought but when the reason for such electronic gadgets hit home she shuddered and decided, *I need to do more to help find the bomber so I can get my life back.*

Tooms let her out of the FBI car in front of Daniel Boone Clinic. He told her to call when she finished and he would take her to get her car and let her practice with her new toy. Susan greeted the receptionist, and in her office glared at the palm pad. The security buttons prompted an image of a rust-haired preacher. "This security is peanuts, Milton. No wonder you have stress headaches, what with all the fancy equipment in the parsonage and the church—yeah, and a constant shadow for a bodyguard."

The patient load was normal and the ailments routine so that Susan felt relaxed by the end of the day. At noon she had asked the nurse assigned to her to bring a hamburger and Coke from McDonald's. While nibbling at the fare she experimented with her new cellular and called Milton. He told her to read the second page of the morning paper, telling her Zinger had attacked him again. They recounted the picnic time in the meadow, which nudged her to tell him about her new security, for car and home, all as a cell phone in a palm pad. Milton's expression of relief at her security was so moving that Susan stirred deep inside. The nurse commented on her new toy.

With a flourish Susan closed the last chart and opened the large yellow envelope she had stuck under her palm pad. An hour before, the receptionist had handed it to Susan, and said the nurse that delivered it said it was confidential. The contents straightened Susan in her swivel chair. She opened the envelope and removed a single sheet of paper. Scribbled at the top of the page was a note:

> Susan—interesting data. The first two paragraphs of
> text and numbers have the data on complication of
> egg harvesting and abortions; the third, the number
> of late-term abortions. I was interrupted during the
> printout of these data so I didn't get the informa-
> tion on embryos. The number penciled in at the
> bottom is the security code to the computer that
> has that data.

Susan examined the number. Below it was a signature, Marion Taswell's. She picked up the palm pad while searching her desk Rolex for Tooms's number. Before she could locate it, she remembered he had said that by punching the pound sign three times in rapid succession she could connect with his wristwatch phone, three times with the star sign would connect with Abel's wristwatch phone. Five seconds and Tooms was on the phone. The sound of his voice reminded her to point the screen at her face.

"Ready, Doctor? Move it closer." She did as instructed and he said, "Better. You don't look too bad for such a long day. I hope they pay you well."

"How soon, Max?"

"Five minutes. I'm on my way from Heiter's. Meet me out front."

Susan turned off the cellular and spying Taswell's envelope, rummaged through a desk drawer and found an old medical journal. She removed the page from the envelope, folded it in half, and stuck it between pages of the journal. With the palm pad in her bag she went out the front door, waving at the male receptionist who worked evenings when the clinic became an urgent care center.

During the drive to get her car at the FBI trailer, Tooms told her Milton was upset with the distortions in Zinger's column and told him it had spawned an interview by CNN. Before he could tell her what the interview revealed, they arrived at the trailer. Susan examined the Chrysler. It looked the same. She stepped closer. A voice barked, "Don't touch. You'll be sorry." She found the palm pad and touched a front fender. The siren, though anticipated, startled her. She fumbled to get the palm pad open and then hit the left top button. Tooms stood by the back bumper, nodding approval, so she next hit the middle button. The doors unlocked. Smiling, she punched the right button. The engine roared to life.

Tooms nodded his head approvingly and said, "I'll follow you to your apartment." He turned for his car but after a few strides turned and yelled, "Wait."

Susan heard him above the sounds of the radio and let down the driver's window. She looked out the window toward Tooms. "In the parking lot across from your apartment—not the space right under your window but across from it—you will find an orange barrel with a reserved sign attached. That's yours. Move aside the barrel—it's plastic, light—and park there." He turned for his car.

In the lot Susan spied the barrel between a white van and a red SUV. She put the car in park, shoved the barrel to one side, and drove in. Climbing out of her car, she watched Tooms park under her apartment window. She headed for the building door.

On the sidewalk Tooms reached her side. "Did you arm it?" He nodded toward her car.

"Rats," Susan said, opened the palm pad, and pushed the left button on the top row. A double beep sounded.

"Good. Those vehicles next to yours are FBI. Come, let me show you the apartment security. Remember what I told you?"

They were inside the building. Susan said, "Certainly." And punched the left button on the second row. She muttered, "Disarmed." But when she tried the door an alarm sounded, seemingly from all directions. She recalled the earlier conversation and quickly hit the second button in the second row, at the same time watching a camera above the front door swing in her direction. "Sorry, Max."

The door to the apartment across from hers flew open and a man stood in the hallway. Max, who had hovered near the front door during the entire episode said, "It's okay, Fetter. Meet Susan Benz, Doctor Benz."

Susan stared at the revolver until the stocky man put it in a holster under his arm. He didn't smile. He had ruddy cheeks, was a couple inches shorter than she. His wide-set eyes and barely visible eyebrows gave him a deadpan look.

"Mat Fetter, Doctor. You'll learn the electronic world we live by," the man said and followed Tooms into the apartment across the hall from Susan's. At Tooms's beckon Susan trailed after him.

"Who lives here?" Susan surveyed the front room. On one wall sat a table with TV monitors and computers. Against another wall was a cache of electronic equipment, unrecognizable by her. A card table with two chairs sat in the middle of the room.

"Fetter and I. We'll be right across the hall. Fetter will man this facility. Don't let him near you, he's woman crazy," Tooms said and went to the door after slapping Fetter on the back.

"Come on, boss. Doc'll believe you." The man turned toward Susan and added, "I was a boxer, not a lawyer like Tooms. I'd sooner punch out a guy than chase a woman."

Susan nodded and followed Tooms to her apartment. He opened the door and stopped in the middle of the living room. Over his shoulder he said to Fetter, who leaned against the doorsill, "Bring three beers from our refrigerator." He waved an arm around the room. "The boys swept the entire place. Found one bug." He fished in his coat pocket and produced a small round black object. As he walked to the front window, he said, "Found this little fella right there." He pulled back the drape on the right and pointed at an upper corner of the picture window. "Put there by someone, probably from this building."

"Could it be cowboy? He lives upstairs." Susan asked disbelievingly.

"Possibly. Guess what? The apartment above this one is empty. The guy vanished, but we'll find him. Might explain how Milton's stalker knew his every move."

Fetter appeared, three beers in his hands. Tooms grabbed two and gave one to Susan after opening it. Susan took a sip and said, "Do you think he's the bomber or spying for the bomber?"

Tooms set his beer on the coffee table. "Bomber. The boys, Mort and Ezrah, told Abel that they only saw the man who gave them the job and paid them, from the waist down, never saw his face. They said the guy wore old weather-worn cowboy boots and a cowboy belt."

Susan said, "A huge black belt with a silver buckle, green cow skull and horns part of the buckle?"

"Exactly. That's what they saw. Didn't see his face," Tooms said.

"Excuse me, boss, but Abel said he got that out of Ezrah, but he's sure they know more. He's going up there tomorrow. Believes with a little cash inducement for their mom, he'll get Mort to describe the guy."

Tooms turned to Susan and said, "You saw the Taswell woman Wednesday. Did she get any data for us?"

Susan peered at the journal she had put under her bag on the coffee table. She wrestled with the answer, afraid that, if the FBI got the data, they might use it in such a way as to expose Taswell. "A little," she lied and sipped beer.

"Any is good. Show me."

Susan squirmed on the opposite end of the couch. Fetter stared with a blank look. "I fear for her, at least her job, if you use the data, Max."

"Come on, we do this all the time. She won't get hurt. They'll never know where we got it," Tooms said.

Reluctantly, Susan removed the paper from the journal and handed it to Tooms. His eyes widened with each paragraph he read. "Wow! Dynamite. We got 'em."

"That's what I was afraid of," Susan moaned.

"No, we will use it to get a search warrant." He motioned to Fetter and said, "Take this and call Judge Bock. Tell him what it says. He'll issue us a search warrant."

Susan watched Fetter take the paper and disappear into the FBI apartment. "Curewell probably knows, may have every judge in their pocket, Tooms. I don't want to betray Taswell's trust."

"Not this one. Judge Bock is a federal judge in Washington, a fine Christian, one who opposes embryos used for stem cell research. He gives the FBI a lot of search warrants, so locals never know how or what information we've got to justify a search."

Susan passed up the offer for dinner at the Mountain View Café, stating she had reading to do. After Tooms left, she opened the paper, searching for Zinger's column. When she discerned that he talked about Milton's Sunday service, she folded the paper and took it into the kitchen. While she ate a bacon-lettuce-and-tomato sandwich she read:

> "The Reverend Heiter did as promised the week before when the property crawled with media, practically every major news service. For some reason there weren't but two local media types other then yours truly at this service, one that proved far more juicy. Heiter spun his usual magic, relying on obtuse Biblical references to convince his captured audience that when an embryo from in-vitro fertilization is placed in another woman's womb, not the egg donor, everyone involved sins. That is known as surrogate pregnancy. Remember, Heiter is a product of in-vitro fertilization but normal pregnancy, not surrogate, so naturally he doesn't consider IVF a sin."

Munching on her BLT, Susan read where Zinger said Heiter called for a confrontation at Curewell, that he had some powerful out-of-state demonstrators coming to make this the most forceful march yet. Susan stuck her tongue out at the paper, and told herself, "He didn't say that." The next part made her gulp an unchewed mouthful of BLT.

> "Following a moment of strange behavior on the preacher's part, the preacher's doctor, Doctor Susan Benz of the Daniel Boone Clinic, walked down the aisle from the back and told the audience she too was a product of in-vitro fertilization. Heiter thanked her for her witness, but the good doctor seemed more interested in the preacher's bizarre behavior. Later, the guy admitted to being tired, but his actions weren't those of somebody tired, or exhausted. Maybe he has a brain tumor, or perhaps his constant charade against

a powerful corporation and their clinic has affected his mind."

Susan finished her sandwich. She picked up her palm pad and dialed her parents' home in Chicago. Her mind pictured the view of their north-side apartment, on Lake Shore Drive. She imagined that from a fifteenth floor window she could see the dark waters of Lake Michigan, a dark silvery surface under the full moon. A click jolted her to the present.

"This is Doctor Benz," a clipped voice said.

"Dad, it's Susan." When she recalled that he had a video-phone, she aimed the palm pad at her face. "How do I look?"

"Well, well, a new toy. They must pay you young docs better than they did in my day. We just talked yesterday. Is anything the matter?"

Shock—when he talked his face appeared on the palm pad screen. "Max didn't tell me," she muttered, and before she could respond, the face on the screen asked, "Who's Max? I thought your preacher friend's first name was Milton."

Surprised again, this time at the sensitivity of the pad, she smiled and said, "A Circuit City clerk. Everything is fine," she lied and, remembering she was on video, forced a smile for the screen. "I thought we should talk without the presence of my friend. Is this a good time?"

"If you don't want him to be more than a friend, what's there to discuss? Didn't you tell me he knows you're an IVF kid, surrogate, and had an abortion?" Susan read the tone to his voice, a seriousness that crept in as he talked.

"Yeah, we've shared many personal things. He is a friend, but his religion and my science keep us from being more than close friends, companions—which fits my career plans perfectly."

"What aspect of that age-old battle do you two disagree about most?"

Susan smiled and waved a finger at the screen. "That's precisely why I wanted to speak to you without him being present.

Being—when is an embryo a being? I told him I didn't harbor guilt over my abortion because a fetus isn't a being. He maintains that a fetus is a being and claims that an embryo, when two DNAs join in fertilization, is a being."

Her father's face had a look that she recognized from early childhood, a didactic look. "Many of us in the neurosciences believe a being is present when the nervous system of the fetus develops, somewhere around the ninth to twelfth week of gestation. Did he give any source for his belief?"

"Yes, a nationally known neurosurgeon, head of neurosurgery at Missouri. Do you know him?"

"That would be Professor Oro, about my age, but he's known for establishing the criteria for brain death. The Missouri legislature adopted his criteria and they were used for transplant donors, eventually for other problems and by many other states," the elder Benz said.

"Milton said this Oro also has said that when two DNAs join they are an embryo. I didn't ask him about the basis for Oro's statement."

"And I imagine your friend is opposed to cloning human embryos, Susan."

"Definitely—vehemently. Not just to make a being—try to improve on God's handiwork, His creation—but also use of clones for research."

She could see the face melt into a series of expressions, ones she recognized as consternation. After a lengthy silence, the face changed, a boyish grin appeared. "If the preacher believes a being exists when two DNAs join, a clone isn't a being because two DNAs don't join." He broke into a big smile. "Got him, Susan. Ask him how a human embryo that's cloned can be a being when two DNAs aren't involved."

*Brilliant*, Susan thought, *My pa's so smart*. She nodded her head up and down and said, "Excellent, Dad. So research on cloned human embryos is okay because scientists aren't torturing, killing a being." Susan let the last words drag out because a problem with the entire concept surfaced in her mind. Just as her father opened his mouth to speak she asked, "If your tenet is true, what do we call such clones? Not human beings. How about humanoids?"

"Very good, Susan. You and Milton should have fun—well, if he's rigid like many clerics, it could end your closeness."

Susan chuckled and said, "I doubt that. He likes me lots. One more question. If human clones aren't beings, do they have souls?"

"Tough one, my bright daughter. Ask Milton. I'd love to hear his answers to these questions."

Susan saw his face turn and tilt downwards as she said, "You need to come see me, meet this interesting man and ask him yourself."

"Susan, it sounds to me like you care more for this preacher than you admit. If you can get over these tough ethical issues, you might find him a good companion. Besides, I ought to have grandchildren sometime. Careers aren't that big a deal."

"Why do all men think career is such a big deal for males and we females should be their incubators, forget our careers?" Susan watched a frown creep over his face as she talked.

"Life, Susan. When you get to be my age, you realize that being a big deal isn't the most important thing. You are more important to me than this overblown career of mine."

Emotions rattled Susan's brain. Competing answers only confused her, so she said, "I love you too, Dad."

"Sorry. My answering service is after me. I accept your invitation. I'll see when I have a free weekend and get back to you. I love you. I miss you lots, Susan."

"I miss you, Dad. Bye," Susan said and closed the palm pad.

After reading two medical journals, she climbed in bed with a nagging thought, *Zinger may work his agenda but his remark about Milton worries me. Those were unusual symptoms of exhaustion or being just plain tired. Could it be a brain tumor?*

Tuesday was Susan's day to cover walk-ins and man the urgent care center. A drizzle set in at nine-thirty and, as expected, brought a run of injuries, minor auto accidents and aches and pains seen on any hot, muggy day in Appalachia. Keeping up with the flow of patients, including sending three more seriously injured to the hospital emergency room, occupied her attention so much she couldn't find time to call Milton, and completely forgot to eat lunch. Fatigue became evident to Susan in the middle of the afternoon. The nurse assisting Susan gave her a chart and told her the man in room two had a rash, probably poison sumac, on his right arm. With her eyes reading the data at the top of the chart, Susan didn't look at the patient until she had sat by the small desk in a corner of the room. Her eyes drifted to the exam table. The hair on the back of her neck bristled. The boots were old, well-worn cowboy boots. Anxiety mounted when her eyes raised and stared at the belt, a black one with a huge silver buckle, adorned with a green cow skull and horns. Susan jumped out of the chair, her heart pounding against her breastbone. At the door she turned and glanced at the quizzical face of the lean clean-shaven man. The nurse left the opposite corner and grabbed Susan's arm.

"Is anything the matter, Doctor?"

Susan fixed her gaze on the man and answered, "No. I just had a bad flashback." The man, she figured him to be in his late twenties, seemed amused by her behavior. She approached the exam table after picking up the chart and said, "Would you mind telling me where you got that belt?" A twinge of embarrassment made her pause. "Very unique. I'm new to Appalachia, learning every day some different type dress."

"I'm a temporary security guard for Curewell—to protect their property during this weekend demonstration," he said. He thrust his right arm in front of Susan. "I got this back in Tennessee a couple days ago—driving me crazy."

"You didn't say where you got the unique belt," Susan persisted.

"When I come here yesterday, the head of Curewell security gave me these here old boots and this belt. Sorta a uniform I guess, because I seen several other temporary security guys with similar boots and belt."

Susan struggled to hide her dismay, her mind prodding her with the problems that made in collaring the bomber. She examined the rash, asked if he had it anywhere else, and wrote on her prescription pad. She tore off the paper and, giving it to the man, studied his eyes. They looked innocent. "That ointment should give you relief. Enjoy your stay in Harlan."

She went to the urgent-care office, sat on the desk chair, and stared out the window. "Curewell uniform same as the bomber. Several temporary security men from out of state. I wonder if Max knows," she said and made a note on the man's chart.

"Only four more, Doctor," the nurse said, standing in the doorway.

Susan managed to keep her attention directed toward patient problems, but more than ever scrutinized every one, analyzing their dress, their behavior and their expressions, each unusual feature feeding a creeping fear.

The day's toll became evident when she leaned against her car and the scolding voice turned into a siren. Half the occupants of the nearby buildings, those still working at five-forty, stared out windows. Susan fumbled in her bag, found the palm pad and hit the first button. She waved at the nearest windows and hit the second button and then the third.

A scruffy looking man, standing by a rusted—out pickup truck two cars away, rubbed his beard and exclaimed, "How'd ya do that, womer?"

*Womer?* Susan thought and opened the door, turned and said, "Magic." After that goof, Susan stopped five feet from her apartment door. Moving the orange barrel to park had been a good reminder, so she hit the first button in the second row of her palm pad and then unlocked the door with the second button. She smiled briefly, paused at her door, her mind poking her memory. She went to the outside door, pulled it ajar, and aimed the palm pad at her car, pushing the first button on the first row. Two beeps told her the car door locked, alarm system armed. She smiled, opened her apartment door, and collapsed on the couch, like a woman on a mission. A glance at her watch told her it was five minutes to six. She grabbed the TV remote and hit four, the local news channel. Kicking off her shoes, she thought, *Milton's interview wasn't on last night. Surely it'll be on tonight.* The local channel's anchor appeared.

"Breaking news right here in Harlan." This is it, she surmised and pulled her legs under her. "Curewell Clinic was shut down by the FBI today. Max Tooms, the agent in charge, refused to give details but this channel has learned that the clinic was closed pending the investigation of their latest report. It seems that in their quarterly report to Washington they stated there were no complications from their abortions or in harvesting eggs for making embryos. But the FBI has found out that the quarterly report was false. They have been here three weeks and somehow found out Curewell has had many complications." While the man talked, pictures of FBI agents posting signs at the front door of Curewell marched across the screen. "While such alleged negligences result in substantial fines, other problems must exist. A source close to me intimated that Curewell has done late-term abortions, a serious offense."

Susan watched the rest of the half-hour, but no mention was made of Milton or his interview. She went into the kitchen and pulled a pizza from the freezer. While the microwave cooked it, she opened a beer and enjoyed the cold liquid as it slid down. She held the cold can against her forehead, imagining it cooled her whole body.

Susan didn't remember when her head hit the pillow. From nowhere a siren jolted her out of a deep sleep. Instantly, she recognized the wailing of her car alarm. She got tangled in the covers rolling out of bed, fought free and, in pajamas, dashed to the front window in the living room. Bright lights illuminated her car and twenty feet in each direction. *No one in sight. Who did that?* she queried under her breath and at that moment saw two men below her window. They had come out of the building's front door. One went to the left and the other to the right, sweeping around toward her car. Once they walked under the bright lights, she recognized Tooms and Fetter, each holding a revolver. Tooms pressed an object in his hand and the siren stopped. Lights from other apartment windows illuminated an eerie scene along the front of the building. Tooms motioned to Fetter and he disappeared into the night. Tooms walked toward the front entrance, but on the sidewalk looked toward her window. She knocked on the glass and waved. He disappeared and a knock sounded on her door. Susan went to the door and looked through the peep window. Tooms smiled at it.

Susan invited Tooms in, covering her chest with her arms before going to the bedroom to get a robe. Tooms was in jogging gear, his hair a mess, his eyes bleary.

"Can I get you something, Max?"

"Beer. And better bring one for yourself, Susan," Tooms said.

Returning with the beer, Susan reflected on the evening news and interrupted Max when he started to ask her if she was all right. "You told me the FBI wouldn't expose Taswell. The evening news anchor certainly had all the information," she flashed her meanest look and waved a finger at him.

"Guilty as charged," he said and swallowed beer. "I didn't tell anyone, and Fetter only gave the data in Taswell's letter to our friendly judge in Washington. He never tells."

"Typical Washington bureaucracy, Max. No one ever tells, but somehow such stuff leaks out and good people get hurt." Susan swished a mouthful of beer around her mouth trying to cool down. She swallowed and in a metered voice said, "Don't ask me to help again. I don't lie to people like the FBI." She stood and with both hands on her hips said, "Good night."

"Sit down, Benz. This isn't some girl scout game we are playing." Tooms tilted the can up, draining the last of the beer. "This afternoon Abel found Mort and Ezrah's bodies at the bottom of the cliff-side road. Someone wanted us to think it was an accident, but forensics determined they were dead when they hit the rocks." He waited as if expecting Susan to ask a question. She fought to contain her anger, remained silent with a cold stare at him. He shrugged his shoulders. "Dead people don't bleed and there was no blood at the crash site. Benz, Heiter was almost killed, and the guy is still out there, cowboy boots, belt and all. He's killed the only persons who could identify him."

Susan waved her hand at Tooms but he misinterpreted her action and added, "Many people are inconvenienced, some have feelings hurt, lose a friend, but often it takes that and more to catch a clever killer. In our search of Curewell, we found many illegal things—that's why we were able to shut them down. And hopefully we will be able to connect them to the attempt on Heiter's life. Think on that before you judge us so harshly."

Susan forced a smile, went to the kitchen and returned with another beer. She handed it to him and said, "Today I had a patient with worn cowboy boots and a belt buckle with green cow skull and horns."

"You should have hit the red button on your palm pad," Tooms said.

"This guy was in his twenties and lean. The real cowboy is older, husky. Today's cowboy told me Curewell gave him boots and belt as uniform as well as to several other temporary security men."

Tooms grimaced and said, "With Mort and Ezrah dead, that gives us an identification problem."

"I can identify the cowboy," Susan said.

Tooms choked on the beer when she told the story of the cowboy's visit to her clinic the week before.

Following this revelation their dialogue was more amicable. As Tooms left he told Susan he would have mug shots from the FBI file for her to look at over lunch hour.

Mixed emotions sent Susan to sleep. With the murder of Mort and Ezrah, she worried more about Milton and felt guilty for involving Taswell. *But without her data we would never implicate Curewell or find the bomber. I can identify the guy, the weird cowboy*, she concluded.

# EIGHT

The storm that brought a drizzle to Baxter all day Tuesday passed, leaving Wednesday morning a steam bath. Milton Heiter smiled as he put the cereal box away, when he realized his headache was hardly noticeable. Yet, the mirror on the back porch showed a strained face. Maybe it's the fresh haircut, he decided and walked across the backyard toward the church, intent on organizing the meeting for Saturday's demonstrators.

"Yo, Pastor," a voice to his left yelled.

Milton turned and waited until Abel strode beside him.

"May I visit with you in your office before you get started on the day's work?" Abel held open the back door to the church.

"Please, come tell me what last night's news about Curewell means. Are they really shut down?" Milton walked into the office and sat behind the desk.

"Were shut down," Abel said as he pulled a chair next to the desk. "A local judge put out a restraining order. They opened for usual business this morning."

Milton was confused. He shook his head from side to side. "How can that be?"

"Politics, Preacher. U.S. senator from this state fixed it," Abel said.

"Why? I thought both senators were conservative."

Sarcasm eked out of Abel when he said, "They want to get reelected, don't they?"

Milton tilted his head but ringing stopped his retort. He picked up the receiver. A smooth voice said, "This is Doctor Cranston Burgess, Reverend Heiter. I would like to come over this afternoon and visit. May I bring the corporation lawyer?"

"Please come and bring whomever you wish. How's three o'clock, in the church office?" After the man said three was okay, Milton told him to enter the front door of the church. "The door to the office is to the left of the narthex," he said, then replaced the receiver in its cradle and looked at Abel. "Burgess and his lawyer are coming at three."

Abel stiffened. "Did he reveal the purpose of the meeting?"

"No, but with his lawyer coming I doubt he wants to have a tea party. Isn't Tooms a lawyer?"

"Many FBI agents are. Tooms doesn't practice, but he'd be good to have at your side. I smell skunk. When I see him at lunch time, I'll tell him you would like to have him in attendance at three," Abel said.

"Is there anything else, Abel?" Milton grabbed the stack of papers that had the names and plans for Saturday's demonstration.

"Late yesterday I found Mort and Ezrah at the bottom of a cliff. Supposed to look like an accident but our forensic expert has concluded that they were killed somewhere else," Abel said.

"That's bad. I don't suppose anybody will be able to identify cowboy. There goes your best lead," Milton said.

"You should know about your doctor. Her close..." Abel paused, studying Milton.

Milton dropped the papers on the desk and said, "I heard that the data that led to the search warrant came from her contact at Curewell—Taswell, I believe. What else should I know?" Milton watched Abel's stone face melt.

"Benz's association." Abel stopped again. "Look, Preacher, I saw you at the meadow. Anybody can see you two care for each other. That means the bomber sees it too. Tooms has set up tight security for Doctor Benz. Her car and apartment have the latest security systems."

"So some thug wants to hold her hostage so he can get to me. This sounds like a TV program my parents watched twenty years ago." Milton's mind sent other messages. Studying Abel's face for the response, he thought, *Two people, now maybe four, have been killed for me already. I don't need more, especially Susan.*

"Sounds as if you watched the same flicks as your parents. No, our number one suspect for the bomber is cowboy. Doctor Benz saw him as a patient. She is scheduled to look at mug shots in our file," Abel said. He leaned toward Milton, projecting his stone face forward. "She can ID the guy. That makes her at extreme risk."

Milton frowned. "Anything else?"

"Nothing more." Abel paused, deep in thought. "Well, one more thing. Many security people are in town—hired by Curewell—and seems most have worn cowboy boots and the same funny cowboy belt."

"You mean same as the bomber suspect?"

"Right. We need to discuss how to handle an encounter when you run into a guy with such attire," Abel said.

"Do? What's there to do?" Milton attempted to conjure up the significance of Abel's revelation, but it got mixed up with worry over Susan.

"You won't know if the one you see is the real cowboy or not, so you must make every attempt to keep your distance from anyone dressed like that. Tonight…" Ringing from the desk phone inter-rupted Abel.

Milton removed the receiver. Susan's voice brought out a huge grin. "My favorite doctor," he said, then covered the mouthpiece with his hand and asked Abel, "Can we talk later?"

"Catch ya before you retire tonight," Abel said and departed.

Milton removed his hand from the mouthpiece. "Sorry. Abel and I were just finishing. He brought me up to date on the recent happenings."

"Did he tell about the cowboy look-alikes?"

"Yes. And the politics that allowed Curewell to open right away." Milton hesitated and said, "Can you come over tonight? I have some great leftovers in the frig. And we can talk about your career—and mine—and ours."

"Ours?"

"Yes. I think you would make a great Professor and Head of Neurosurgery—and a great mother. Men juggle careers and kids."

"I'd love to come over and dissect this topic, but I promised Tooms I would look at the rest of the mug shots after dinner. I saw a few over lunch hour. None looked like cowboy. Thursdays are my usual afternoon free. How about I come over around two?"

Milton's glum feeling gave way to a feeling of joy and antici-pation. "Perfect. You can help me tidy up the last of the plans for Saturday's march, and we can work on my confusion."

Susan chuckled and said goodbye.

After lunch Milton took two aspirin and lay down on the bed, intending to rest fifteen minutes. A hand squeezed his shoulder and extracted him from a pleasant conversation with his seminary ethics professor. He opened an eye and looked into the smiling face of Tooms. "Sorry, but Burgess and his lawyer are waiting for you in the church office. You feel up to it? I could cancel for you."

Milton swung his feet over the edge of the bed and ran a hand through his rust-colored hair. "I'm fine. Just a bit tired, a brief rest." A glance at his watch told him it was ten after three, not a fifteen-minute rest. Passing through the kitchen, he saw a note on the table. It was written on a prescription form:

> Milton
> You were sleeping so soundly I didn't wake you—
> you need the rest. Call later.
>
> Susan

He followed Tooms to the church, angry that he had missed Susan. In the office, a graying, older man in a white coat stood, studying the certificates on the office wall. A lean man in a three-piece, light blue summer suit sat next to the desk. He turned and stood, his tan face with gray-blue eyes framed by wavy, deep brown hair. The immaculate dress told Milton he was the attorney. The man extended a hand. Milton took it, feeling a vise-like grip.

"Reverend Heiter, I recognize you from your pictures in the papers and TV. They don't do justice to you. I'm Carlisle Burford, Curewell corporate attorney."

The man in the white coat turned around as Milton said, "Kind of you, counselor." He turned toward the other man. "You must be Doctor Burgess? Please be seated."

Burford returned to the chair beside the desk while Burgess pulled a chair from the wall and moved it next to Burford. Burgess sat, his stiff composure unchanged. "Thank you for seeing us. We wanted…" He stopped when Tooms arrived and pushed a chair next to Milton's desk chair. "Agent Tooms, you do get around," Burgess said with an icy tone that the August heat couldn't melt.

Burford smiled and reached a hand across the desk to Tooms. "Agent Tooms, I've heard many things about your work with the Bureau. Are you here as Heiter's attorney? It isn't necessary."

Milton watched Tooms unbutton the jacket that was about to pop a button and loosen his tie. His demeanor was entirely different from that Milton recognized. His eyes had a penetrating glare, unwavering as they pounced on Burgess's face and then rested on Burford's. In a metered voice he said, "I am not here as Pastor's attorney, but since Burgess has a legal here, I thought the Reverend might need legal input."

"Very nice of the FBI. A good starting point. What Curewell does is legal," Burford said.

Tooms waved a hand at Heiter when he opened his mouth to speak and spoke to Burford. "Let's all understand what you just said. At the end of the last century the most crucial statement about using embryos for research came from the Tennessee Supreme Court."

Burford put on his plastic smile and said, "They concluded that pre-embryos were neither person nor property. They occupy an intermediate category. So Curewell is within its legal right to…"

Tooms turned his gaze on Milton, generated a warm smile, and told him, "Burford wasn't going to tell you the crucial part of their conclusion. The court said that pre-embryos occupy an intermediate category that entitles them to special rights because of their potential for human life, and said rights of progenitors are supreme."

"Well," Burford said, stiffening in his chair and glancing at Burgess, "Clinton and the conservatives used that and fear of public reaction to restrict use of embryos for research. Then…"

"And denied hundreds of people the chance of benefiting from a cure of disease that our research would have found," Burgess said in a too-loud voice.

"The chance—might have—the potential for-possibly might-and so on, Doctor," Milton said. He paused, but Burgess just frowned. "Years later—a different century— you guys still say the possibles, the mights, the could haves. You've cured few if any and produced monsters, murdered thousands of little beings."

Tooms nodded at Milton. Burgess turned red. Burford stood and, standing behind the doctor, squeezed both shoulders. "Emotional tripe, Heiter. Eighteen months ago President Campbell signed into law the use of embryos for research."

"And still we wait for all these miracles that possibly might come from the heinous research," Milton said.

"You and dying patients wait because do-gooders like you, Heiter, stopped progress for ten years," Burgess said and made eye signals to Burford.

"And the Christian Medical and Dental Society, as they did when this began ten years ago, has filed a suit—this one in the Supreme Court of the United States challenging the law that has made a travesty of our Christian faith," Milton said.

Burford returned to his seat while Tooms made a time-out signal with his hands and said, "I am here also for Milton's protection."

Milton noticed that he punched a button on the side of his wristwatch. Milton smiled to himself, for he knew from other encounters that Tooms had just switched his watch to broadcast mode—to the trailer.

Burford opened his mouth but before he could speak, Burgess spewed, "Insulting. Are you insinuating that his meeting with us requires protection?"

"Easy, Cranston," Burford said, his smooth, mellow voice matching his posture and countenance. "With another march scheduled in three days and the violence anticipated with it, we have contracted for increased security." His smile faded. "And with the bombing of Pastor's house they have as much reason to think he needs protection."

Milton studied the interplay and said, "FBI thinks I need protection. I think the whole business is overdone." He turned his gaze on Burford. "Violence against Curewell at the last demonstration was from outsiders. I marched my people back here. We are nonviolent. Legal..."

Burford had donned his supercilious smile. "Of course, Reverend. During the protests against abortion clinics ten years ago you people who abhor the killing—I think you characterize abortions as murders—killed those at such clinics—those who had legal right to do abortion."

Milton squirmed in his seat and said, "I don't condone murder in any form and that goes for the antiabortion people who resort to violence to protest." He smiled at Burford.

"Of course, you don't condone such violence that has led to death at abortion clinics." Milton saw Tooms start to speak, but Burford waved a finger at him. "But those murders occurred and the violence at your last demonstration here in Harlan occurred because you incite participants to violence."

Milton took a deep breath, formulating a biblical response when Tooms said, "Garbage, Counselor. We could just as well say Burgess incited it by the abortions in his clinic and his creating of little ones to be murdered by research." Milton saw fire in Burford's eyes and a hissing came from Burgess. Tooms loosened his tie further and continued. "Violence two weeks ago was a complication of legal protests just as the complications Burgess has from legal abortions and harvesting of eggs." Tooms huffed, "The reason Curewell was shut down."

"Was shut down," Burford said and flashed a huge smile. "And Curewell wasn't shut down because of complications, a normal consequence of surgical interventional procedures, Agent Tooms. Curewell was shut down because some incompetent secretary forgot to include the last page of the report, the one with the complications."

"And the late-term abortions, Mr. Burford?"

"We don't do them. Let me remind you that abortions have been legal for forty years. The use of embryos for research has been legal for eighteen months. Your evidence for performance of late-term abortions was hearsay. That's why District Judge Rush overruled the local order."

"Come on. He overruled because a state politician told him to," Tooms said.

Burford removed a paper from an inside coat pocket and gave it to Milton. "The reason we came here was to try to dissuade you from holding the demonstration this Saturday and save a lot of turmoil, maybe injuries."

Milton read the paper and turned to Tooms as he handed it to him. "Judge Rush says we must keep at least fifty yards from the clinic property."

Tooms handed back the paper after reading it and said, "Perfectly legal, Milton."

Burgess had moved to the edge of his chair, a scowl on his face. "I would think, Heiter, that after someone bombed your house, you would avoid exposure like this Saturday. Next time it could be a sniper." He finished with a smirk.

"A threat..." Tooms blurted but Burford stopped him.

"Cranston wasn't threatening, just worried," Burford said. "We have men who are as eager to protect the Reverend's right to protest, but you've seen the herd of people that came into town this week and more will come by Saturday. Reverend Heiter, I'm certain it was not pastors like you who bombed the clinic in Atlanta and killed the doctor's nurse. What worries Cranston is that just as you can't control violent elements that join you, we can't be responsible if some pro-abortion nut aims a high-powered rifle at you."

Out of the corner of his eye, Milton saw the disgust creep over Tooms's face, so he moved a hand toward him, but looked at Burford. "I appreciate your concern." Milton looked at Burgess and said, "If God needs me upstairs now, so be it. What I have done, I am ready to be judged by God Almighty. I hope you are, Doctor Burgess." Milton's dull ache now pressed on him. Nausea stopped further cogitations.

"Goodbye, gentlemen." He rose and left the church, heading for the parsonage kitchen and the aspirin bottle.

A brief rest on the bed rejuvenated Milton. He splashed cold water on his face and went to the kitchen. Though the nausea had disappeared, he had little appetite. Spying two pieces of pizza left over from the night before, he put them in the microwave. After a couple of bites, downed with iced tea, Abel appeared in the doorway of the kitchen.

"You might want to bring your pizza and catch the five-thirty news. The local affiliate of NBC just announced that in the next half-hour they would air the interview with the Reverend Milton

Heiter, leader of the upcoming march against the embryo factory in Harlan, Kentucky," Abel said and turned for the living room.

Milton grabbed a tray, deposited his pizza and tea on it, moved to the TV, and sat on the recliner facing the TV set. "Anything else about Curewell, about their closing?"

"Yeah," Abel said. "They told the viewers about us shutting them down and alluded to the role of politics in reopening."

Both men turned silent when the channel anchor said, "All of Harlan trembles over the upcoming protest march. Anticipating violence, perhaps more severe than three weeks ago, Curewell has hired a squad of security police." While he talked, scenes from the last demonstration showed protestors breaking into Curewell Clinic and the melee that followed. "The situation in Harlan is volatile. The streets look like a Fourth of July weekend, jammed with people from organizations representing both sides of the abortion and stem cell issues. We have been told that NOW, Pro-choice and others plan a demonstration in front of Rev. Heiter's house in Baxter tomorrow afternoon. A spokesperson for the organizations said that Heiter kills adults everyday by impeding research using embryo stem cells. She said that if the use of embryo stem cells hadn't been prohibited by the likes of Heiter and the Pro-life crowd, science would probably have cures for many fatal diseases that kill Americans everyday, hundreds more than terrorism."

A red-cheeked face of a woman appearing to be in her fifties filled the screen. She said, "Good point. Yes, a few of our people might agree with the reverend that embryos are beings. But if so— I personally do not believe an embryo is anything but property— anyhow, if so, using them for stem cell research is the lesser of two evils. Because millions of people, children and adult beings who already enjoy life, who have a full life ahead of them, are snuffed out by diabetes, cancer, heart disease, and thousands of others crippled, suffer immeasurably from disease and injuries of the nervous system. And all of these poor souls leave grieving loved ones. Embryos don't suffer. They don't leave loved ones behind. No one grieves, because embryos are nothing, have been nothing."

The anchor's face returned to the screen. "Now that is a logical, impelling presentation, one that must make the Heiters of the world fish for a response. In fact, our national network interviewed the good pastor two days ago. Here are excerpts from that interview made by Katherine Hardin. We don't take sides. We present the news, both sides of the issues."

Milton leaned forward in the recliner as the face of an attractive blonde woman, the one who interviewed him, filled the screen. "So you say that you are against stem cell research, Reverend Heiter. Don't you feel compassion for people with diabetes, cancer, and other fatal diseases that might be cured by stem cell research?"

"Wrong," Milton shouted at the TV. "I told her I was against the use of embryos for stem cell research, and I encouraged the use of stem cells from cord blood and adults."

He eased back in the chair as the voice continued. Finally, the screen showed his face puckering at the camera as he said, "You misquoted me, but I noted that you said stem cell research might cure all those diseases. Ten years ago, when this debate started, you people said, and the scientists pleaded, for killing of God's littlest beings by shrieking that same emotional harangue. The media kept hawking that research from embryo stem cells might, it could, it probably would lead to cure of cancer and every disease that strikes fear in the heart of man."

The pretty face popped on the screen. Hardin smiled and with a warm voice spoke into the microphone. "And you don't believe we still must say embryo stem cell research might lead to cures because the far-right Christians like you held back progress—at least until eighteen months ago?"

The camera shifted to Milton's stern face as he said, "I don't see any sign on my lapel that says I'm a far-right Christian." He held a Bible between his face and the camera. A camera from a different view captured his face, an angle that did not show the

Bible. "If I'm far right, so is Jesus, because I live and preach by His word."

His face faded into the distance, but the voice of the woman said, "Clearly, my last question was too tough for the Reverend Milton Heiter to handle."

"I answered. They chose not to let the viewers hear it—so much for fair and balanced news. Thanks, Abel," Milton said and left, throwing over his shoulder, "I'm not sure that distorted, edited interview is good for my health."

Milton's head throbbed, nausea returned. For three hours he worked at the kitchen table, attempting to repress the TV picture that threatened to make his head explode. Slowly, he solidified plans for the march and began to draft options if violence or creditable threats of violence preceded Saturday's march.

A quiet cough raised his head. In the doorway stood Abel, dressed in cleric garb, exactly the kind worn by Milton. Shirt, and rust-colored hair kept Milton's mouth agape.

"You shaved your mustache. Trying to take my job?" he exclaimed.

After Abel turned around as if modeling the latest fashion, he said, "Not your job. But I hope from a distance I'm mistaken for you."

"You'll more likely convince everyone if you carry a Bible." Milton smiled when Abel growled.

"Don't think..." Abel stopped when his wristwatch barked, "Code gray on TV." Abel spun around and dashed for the living room. Within a minute he reappeared in the kitchen, a smile on his face.

"False alarm. Relax. The sensors," he pointed toward the roof, "picked up movement out back and the night eyes caught a figure." He chuckled while he walked to the back kitchen window and added, "Your friend Jethroe didn't listen to you. He's the one, bib-overalls and..."

Like a hungry bobcat Milton sprang out of the chair and threw himself at Abel. The impact of his blow against Abel's back was accompanied by the sound of shattering glass. Milton landed on Abel. Glass fragments showered them. Abel moaned in between four-letter words.

"I sent Jethroe to Mozelle to get placards, Hank," Milton said and started to ask Abel where he was hit when he felt warm sticky fluid on his hand that nestled Abel's shoulder. Withdrawing his hand, he stared at the blood. Abel groped for his wristwatch, found it and punched a button. Through clenched teeth he said, "Tell 'em."

Milton leaned toward the watch but stared at the blood oozing out of several spots on Abel's face. He spoke into the watch, "Abel's shot bad. Call 911 and…"

Abel interrupted, yelling, "Code one."

Milton said, "That figure isn't Jethroe. He left Baxter three hours ago."

The watch came to life. "Stay down, help is on the way. Don't move Abel. We'll start a diversion from here." Suddenly, the house became dark and light from the backyard burst through the glassless window and the door, bright as the mid-day sun. Milton heard a snarling, barking dog. It seemed to come from the back porch. He removed his shirt, rolled it in a ball and pressed against the growing bloody spot on Abel's shoulder. Racing motors and gravel sounds hit his ears. Footsteps on the front porch stiffened him.

"Relax. Stay down. Trailer fixed all this. That's the boys." Abel reached with his free arm and produced a gun. From the projected backyard light Milton could see Abel's contorted face as he handed Milton the 38. If they don't say FBI, shoot the first body that comes through the door. Rattling at the front door sounded as Abel said, "Quick response, take the damn thing and shoot."

Milton shoved the gun away. "I can't shoot anyone. I don't…"

"FBI," a harsh voice said from the living room and a figure with an automatic rifle sprang into the kitchen. "Abel, it's Conrad."

Sirens sounded from the direction of Harlan. Milton saw the night vision gear and suddenly felt weak. The man hovered over them when a second voice, this one from the back porch, yelled, "FBI."

"Conrad here. Got both our guys secure." Dying sirens sounded out front. "Go get the medics here."

The man from the porch, also wearing night vision gear and carrying an automatic rifle, stepped over Milton and went toward the living room. A voice out back hollered, "All clear out here, Conrad." Conrad spoke into an object in his hand and the house lights came on. A hand pulled up Milton. A man in a white shirt and trousers cut off Abel's shirt and began to apply a pressure dressing as another medic started an intravenous in the opposite arm. A stretcher appeared. They eased Abel onto the stretcher and disappeared out the front. A hand turned Milton. He stared into the eyes of a man with a crew cut. His eyes shined blue in the glare of the kitchen lights. The young face expressed warmth and concern. He proceeded to pick glass fragments from Milton's hair and asked, "You alright?"

"I don't hurt," Milton said.

"Is he hurt, Conrad?" A familiar voice sounded from the back porch.

"Doesn't appear to be," Conrad said.

Milton looked at Tooms as he approached from the porch. Tooms took Milton's hand and led him into the bedroom.

"Strip to your skivvies, Milton. We need to be sure."

Milton stripped to his boxer shorts. Tooms slowly looked over Milton's front, turned him around and did the same to his back. Through his short hair he felt Milton's scalp.

"Not a scratch, my good pastor," Tooms said, beaming at Milton. "Tell me what happened. Couldn't have been thirty seconds after we asked Abel to check the TV monitor that we got the Code one."

"Couple hours before then, Abel called me in to watch the local channel play my interview," Milton said.

"Wasn't that a cock-eyed joke? Remember, I was nearby when they interviewed you," Tooms said.

"I worked at the kitchen organizing the plans for Saturday's march when Abel appeared in the kitchen doorway. Clever man. Cleric garb, no mustache, and rust-colored hair surprised me." Milton sat and pulled on his socks and shoes. He stood and continued, "He was telling me how he hoped he might pass for me when his wrist radio told him to check the TV—code gray, I think."

"Yes, monitor in the van spied a figure slinking at the back of the church property," Tooms said.

"Abel reappeared with a smile and said the figure was Jethroe, bib-overalls and all. The next image raised Milton's voice a decibel. "That remark hit me. I had sent Jethroe to Mozelle three hours before. Without thinking, I hurled myself at Abel and tackled him waist high as the window glass exploded on us." Milton followed Tooms back to the kitchen where he watched Tooms survey the window and turn to a man in white coveralls digging into the wall opposite the window.

"Two missed," the man said and held two deformed bullets between gloved fingers.

A man in the doorway to the porch said, "Tracks where the shooter waited—cowboy boots, looks like. We found three casings. 'Pears to be the same caliber that killed the Brown boys."

Tooms gave Milton a bear hug. "Thanks. You saved Abel's life." He made a wry smile. "So now Hank knows his masquerade as the Reverend Heiter works. Tough test."

Milton's throbbing head sent him to the cabinet, where he fished out two aspirin. From the bedroom door Tooms told him he would take Abel's spot on the futon. He yelled after the disappearing Tooms, "Who's looking after Susan?" He clutched his head.

"Fetter is in the apartment across the hall from hers. Besides, she has a magnificent security system. Sleep tight. Susan is safe as at Fort Knox."

Milton opened one eye and then the other. The sun sent silvery beams across the room, making flitting spotlights on the mirror. Knock-knock. Again, but more insistent.

"Yeah," Milton said.

"Pastor! It's nine-thirty. You okay?"

Milton recognized Jethroe's whining voice. "Come in, Jethroe." He mustered enough energy to sit on the edge of the bed. He rubbed his eyes, thinking, *Nine-thirty and still tired.* The door opened and Jethroe entered the bedroom.

"Sorry to disturb you," Jethroe said.

"Did you get the placards?" Milton stood, grabbed blue denim trousers from the back of the chair and slipped them on.

"Got 'em. And I made coffee for you." Jethroe turned for the kitchen.

Milton pulled on a white polo shirt on the way to the kitchen. Approaching the table, he spied the three-foot-square placards. Jethroe handed him a cup of coffee.

"I haven't slept so late for ages," Milton said and flipped through the placards. "I think last night tuckered me out."

"I heard," Jethroe said. He pointed to the glassless window. "I already got glass fer it from the hardware."

Milton grabbed a piece of bread from the refrigerator and nibbled on it. "After you fix the window, would you mount these on the sticks I showed you yesterday?"

Jethroe nodded and watched Milton. "Want I should fix you better victuals?"

"No. I don't have much of an appetite." He watched Jethroe turn for the living room, beckoned by the ringing phone.

Jethroe appeared in the doorway and said, "Doctor Benz on the phone."

Milton's lethargy faded with that announcement. In the living room he picked up the receiver. "Hi Susan," he said and paused to dig up a subject that wouldn't worry her. "You should have awakened me yesterday afternoon. Did you identify the cowboy on any mug shots?"

"None of them looked like him."

"So if he isn't in the FBI file, he must be an amateur, not a professional?" Milton realized this conversation wasn't heading for pleasant dialogue.

"Milton, you can't hide what goes on at your place any more than I can keep from you what happens here. Poor Fetter told me last night about Abel, and another attempt on your life. I'm so happy you weren't hurt. I saw Abel this morning before clinic started. Got his arm in a sling. Probably go home today."

"Poor Fetter? I thought you said he was an ex-fighter, toughest guy of the entire crew. Tooms has been on the phone since I woke up," he said and then sighed. "Last night tuckered me out some. I slept until almost ten, so I don't know what's occupied Tooms's attention."

"I do. I think pandemonium hit the crew this morning after the shooting at your place. I know they've contacted Home Security in Atlanta to send help," Susan said.

"What happened this morning? Someone try again to hit Abel?"

"No, and they weren't trying to hit him last night at your place. My place this morning," she said. The phone was silent. He could hear background noises coming from her phone, a doctor paged, a woman calling out names, usual clinic sounds.

"Tell me, Susan. You still there?"

"I'm here. Oh, Milton, I'm frightened. At seven-thirty this morning I opened my apartment door to go to work. I noticed that the FBI apartment door—you remember it's right across the hall from mine—well, it was wide open. That struck me as being strange. I called out Fetter's name, but as soon as I did that, I had an ominous feeling. I hit the button of my palm pad and opened my door. As I shut the door I looked at their open door and saw a man with cowboy boots."

"You mean the kind cowboy wears—old, beat up. What about the belt?"

"I slammed the door shut and threw the switch for the bar lock that sets the alarm. The alarm sounded. It goes off when someone touches the doorknob."

Milton realized he was strangling the receiver. The more excited Susan's voice became, the harder he squeezed. "Did you get a look at the guy—through the door peep hole?"

"Didn't because I was preoccupied trying to hit the red button on my palm pad. I hit it. The crew in the trailer are magnificent. Before I could say anything, they spoke over my palm pad. 'Quick thinking, Doctor. We got him on the front door camera. Looks like the cowboy you described to us. Teams are on the way. Go have a cup of coffee, but tell us how you knew he was in the hall.' I told them how I found their door open and my instinctive reaction. As I talked I could hear them directing an ambulance for my place and alerting the teams that Fetter might be hurt."

"If Tooms is here, Abel in the hospital, and Fetter..." he hesitated, afraid to ask the suppressed question. "Is Fetter okay? What did they find in the apartment?"

"They found Fetter unconscious. When a team arrived I went over and checked him before the ambulance arrived. Probably a concussion, but not shot."

"So, I was asking if he and Abel are out of commission, who is your protection?"

"One of their lab guys escorted me to the clinic and sits in my office. I think Abel will be at your place by supper, and then Tooms said he will stay across the hall from me," Susan said.

"Could your bodyguard bring you over here later this afternoon? We need to console each other, need to be together, to talk serious."

"First, tell me how you feel. Sleeping until ten isn't normal, even with the wild night you had. And then a long afternoon nap. Tell me. Are the headaches worse?"

Milton pondered the answer. The sunlight disappeared. The bright blue color that he and Susan had painted on the living room walls turned gray. The phone shook in his hand. A vise clamped his head. Nausea made his head swim, or was the room spinning?

"Milton!" He heard Susan's voice scream from the receiver just after it banged on the floor. He told himself to pick it up. But his arm would not move. Instead the floor came to him. The end table lamp bounced off his shoulder. Before darkness and silence engulfed Milton, he heard a fading voice cry out his name.

Chapter

# NINE

The sound of the receiver hitting a hard object made Susan jump, her mind flashing back to the time, when in the pulpit, Milton dropped the coin and then the water glass. She screamed out his name. The guttural sounds that emitted from her palm pad made her cringe. "I wish he had a video-phone," she blurted, but at the same time fearful of what it might have shown. A patient and the clinic nurse stopped in the doorway to her office. Susan waved them on and heard a thud, the sound of a body, and the sound of some object crashing.

"Milton," she screamed and vaulted from behind her desk. Holding the palm pad as she ran out the clinic door, she dodged bodies and ignored the questions, as she ran for the convertible. She punched 911 and told the person who responded to send an ambulance to Reverend Heiter's house in Baxter. She managed to hit the first button and the second on the top row just as she reached the car. Her heart raced. Professional mode seized the moment. She removed her hand from the door handle, backed away ten feet and hit the third button. The engine started. Susan smiled and climbed in. The four miles to Baxter seemed like a hundred. Her mind conjured up various scenarios, all bad. Halfway there she remembered the red button and hit it. Without pointing the palm pad at her face she told it she was heading for Heiter's and then told the voice that kept trying to interrupt about the event that led to her race to Baxter.

Susan drove through the church parking lot, over the grass and to the front door. She vaulted out of the convertible, grabbed her medical bag off the back seat, and mounted the steps two at a time. Jethroe kneeled over a lifeless body on the living room floor. He pleaded for Milton to answer. Milton remained silent. Susan fished in her bag for a pharyngeal airway as she approached. Reflexively, her mind took her through the proper order for managing unconscious trauma victims; *establish airway, stop bleeding, treat shock, call for help and diagnose.* With the airway inserted into Milton's mouth, she felt for a radial pulse, noting the sudden movement of air around the airway. Milton's chest moved easily, but he remained unresponsive.

Jethroe sat on his haunches and stared, a frightened bunny rabbit face. "Did you see anyone? Did he fall?" Susan asked but kept her eyes on the still body, scrutinizing it from head to toe for signs of blood or misaligned extremity.

"I didn't see nobody. After I answered yer ringin', I went to the kitchen and told Pastor. I started to fixin' the kitchen winder when I heard a crashin' sound and found him like this here," Jethroe said.

"And didn't see anyone? Anything suspicious?" Susan realized that was a redundant question for in addition to surveying the form she had quickly felt for abnormalities, front and back.

"Nuthin', Doc," Jethroe said. He stood and picked up the lamp from the floor and placed it on the end table.

Susan stared at a lump, the size of a plum, on Milton's left eyebrow. She noted the slight discoloration and decided it had not increased in size since her arrival.

When she leaned closer and gently examined the orbital ridge for deeper trauma, Jethroe said, "That there bump makin' him sleep?"

Susan searched in her bag and removed the ophthalmoscope, chiding herself for not being a better student when the eye professor instructed the students how to use the instrument to look into the eyes of patients. Momentarily, she ignored Jethroe's question and quizzed herself. *Headaches, nausea, twitching of right extremities and left face, means the patient has a left-sided brain lesion. Examine the good—the right eye—first,* she decided. Kneeling, she leaned close to Milton's face.

As Jethroe queried her about the cause of the problem, she retracted the right eyelid with her free hand and shined the light into Milton's eye. Ignoring the car sounds on the gravel parking lot she looked through the ophthalmoscope, scanning the retina, especially looking to see if the optic nerve was swollen. *Normal,* she concluded and scooted over to Milton's left side, ignoring the footsteps on the front porch and those approaching from the rear hallway.

She bent over, retracted the eyelid and was about to shine the light into Milton's left eye when a male voice announced, "We're Medact. We'll take over."

From her kneeling position, Susan straightened and threw a belligerent look at the paunchy man in all white. "No, you won't. I'm Doctor Benz and you'll not take over. You'll do as I say or go over to the chapel and pray for your job." She leaned close to Milton's face again, and after retracting the eyelid, shined the light through the left pupil. The light moved across the back of the eyeball. Susan set the focus on the red blood vessels that shined through the retina and then slowly moved it to the optic nerve. The difference in the focus between the retinal vessels and the optic nerve confirmed what she had suspected.

"As I suspected," she mumbled, leaned back and turned her face to the fidgeting man in white. "His left optic nerve is swollen from increased intracranial pressure." Susan stopped and smiled at the sound of a fast approaching vehicle. "Pressure in his head gave him headaches, made him sick, made him twitch, sleepy and finally caused him to pass out." She paused to analyze the auto sounds coming from the back of the house. *FBI. Hope it's...*

"Doctor Benz." Tooms interrupted her thought process and fulfilled her wish. "What's Milton's problem?"

Ignoring Tooms, she glared at the medic. "Put an oxygen mask on the patient. Can you start an intravenous?" she said, carefully speaking with a doubting tone, hoping to humble the ambulance jockey.

He got the message and replied, "Yes, Doctor. Which arm? Is isotonic saline okay?"

"Fine. Secure it well and then give forty milligrams of lasix IV push." She searched his shirt, spied the name tag and decided to reward the man for understanding his role in the saga. "I appreciate your rapid response. Can you put him in twenty degrees reversed Trendelenberg?"

"Easy, if we can put him on the stretcher," the man answered.

"Good idea. Use whichever arm has the best forearm vein," Susan said, stood and turned to Tooms, speaking loud enough for both ambulance attendants to hear. "Milton has increased intracranial pressure, more on the left than right. I figure the blow on the back of his head three and a half weeks ago made a contra coup subdural hematoma."

Tooms watched the men move Milton onto a stretcher, one placing a mask on his face while the other started an IV in Milton's left arm. He rested a hand on Susan's shoulder. "Tell me about a contra coup."

"The brain is encased in a sac with fluid so it is cushioned in the rigid skull. This helps absorb some of the force from blows to the head." Susan formed a fist with her left hand and held it an inch from her concave right hand. "Hit the back of my left fist, Max," she said.

He did as instructed, gently, and she told him, "See my fist, Milton's brain, is forced against my palm, his skull, opposite from the point of your blow. So three weeks ago he was struck on the right back of his head and that mashed his brain against the left front. When the brain recoils from striking the skull it can rupture some of the small vessels. They ooze blood between the skull and the brain, making a blood clot. That's called a subdural hematoma, a blood clot under the dura, the membrane of the brain. As it ages it draws in fluid, increasing in size and increasing pressure on the brain."

"So that's why his headaches got worse," Tooms said.

Susan nodded her okay when the paunchy one motioned they were ready to transport Milton to the emergency room. While she spoke to Tooms she punched in the emergency room number on her palm pad. "Increased pressure made him nauseated, somnolent, and irritated the motor strip, the part of the brain that moves muscles, so he got the twitches." Out of habit she moved the palm pad screen in front of her face when the emergency room nurse asked her the problem. "This is Doctor Benz. An ambulance is on the way with the Reverend Heiter. He is unconscious from a subdural hematoma. He has an IV and received 40 milligrams of lasix IV push. Please see that he is maintained in reverse Trendelenberg and is kept on oxygen by face mask."

"Is there anyone you want me to call?" the voice from the pad asked.

"Yes, thank you. Call the radiologist and ask…tell him I want a CT scan of the brain immediately—cancel the elective he's doing. If he can't do that have him call me—you have my pager number. I want strong reasons for him to refuse to do Heiter now."

"Should I put a call into neurosurgery?"

"No." Susan ended the call and held the palm pad at arm's length, putting a hand in front of Tooms when he started to speak.

Her memory bank produced the number to the University of Kentucky Medical Center. When the center operator responded, she asked for Doctor Horace Wilson. Waiting, she looked at Tooms and said, "UK will send a chopper for Milton. I want him to go there because they do the new microsurgery for brain problems." She pointed an index finger at two spots over her left temple. "Two little drill holes and they remove the blood clot."

"How long do you think he'll be there? Is the hospital security up to speed? Any residual?" Tooms rattled off the questions while Susan listened for Wilson to respond.

"Three days, Max. Security department is excellent." Rustling noise emitted from the palm pad. She quickly added, "No residual, usually. Up and about, normal in two days. Back to preaching in a week."

"This is Doctor Wilson. Is this the young Doctor Benz, the one that won't come be my resident?" A raspy voice asked from the pad.

Susan held the phone before her face and said, "I want to come talk about that. And I want you to do me a favor. Send the chopper to Harlan. I have a man with a subacute subdural, a contra coup from a blow to the back of his head three and a half weeks ago. As we speak he's getting a CT scan of his head."

"Can do, depending on his condition."

"His symptoms have been progressive over the past two weeks. He passed out this morning. He has papilledema, the left optic nerve is more swollen than the right. I gave him forty milligrams of lasix IV push—reverse Trendelenberg and on face mask. Anything else? I want you to do your miracle microsurgery, Doctor Wilson." Susan started for the front porch, motioning for Tooms to follow.

"Very good, Benz. Your pa would be proud. What's his state of consciousness and vitals since the lasix."

Susan climbed in the convertible while she listened to Wilson. "Vitals normal. He wasn't conscious when he left for the ER, but began to stir," she said and watched Tooms dash toward the back of the house.

"That's good. The delay in getting him here is safe," Wilson said while Susan hit a button on the pad and started the engine. The sound of the motor made her shudder, for she realized she had entered the car and started the motor without observing the cautions Tooms had drilled in her. Smiling, she backed the car off the yard and decided the stalker wouldn't venture so close to Heiter's house in broad daylight. She headed for Harlan as Wilson continued speaking, "I'll send the chopper. Have him ready to go. Give him another forty milligrams of lasix IV push in an hour, and when you get to the ER, have them start a hydrocortisone drip—same IV. Hang a thousand milligrams in small volume and run it in over thirty minutes. That should get him here. You ride along and call me if his condition deteriorates."

On the way to Appalachian Regional Hospital, Susan glanced in the mirror and noticed Tooms's car, following at a distance. She closed her palm pad as she parked in the emergency room space for ER doctors. As she approached the reception desk, an ER nurse holding a phone to her ear motioned to the back right. Susan stepped into a back exam room, noticing first that a plastic bag with several ounces of urine hung on a lower railing of Milton's bed. She smiled for that meant lasix had already caused the kidneys to dump a lot of body fluids. A face mask was hooked to oxygen and an IV dripped slowly. She recognized the nurse taking the blood pressure.

"Hi, Taswell. Run that IV as slow as you can make it—just to keep it open—after the piggy-back with the hydrocortisone is in." Benz moved to the side of the stretcher.

"Will do, Doctor Benz, and his vitals are fine. He has had a couple lucid spells," Taswell said.

Susan felt his radial pulse, strong and at ninety per minute. She liked that. "When is the CT..."

Taswell threw an index finger toward the door to Susan's right. Susan turned and spied an orderly. "Hi, Doctor Benz," the small, thin man said. "Your patient's next. Doctor Berensen wants you to come along and give him some info."

In radiology Susan put on her best face for the surly radiologist who acted as though he had moved Heiter into the CT room ahead of the president of the United States. With her information, the nasty-behaving man reduced the number of pictures to be taken. Susan waited in the viewing room and used the time to call Guthrie and tell her about Milton. Guthrie said she would catch the next plane available from O'Hare for Louisville or Cincinnati and see Susan that night.

A radiology technician summoned Susan to the CT monitor room. Without looking up or saying a word, Berensen pointed to a chair next to him. He stared at the large monitor in front of them. The subdued lighting in the narrow room made the shadows on the large screen quite distinct. Past the monitor she caught a glimpse through the observation window of the technician taking Milton from the CT room.

"Left frontal subdural extending posteriorly to impinge on the motor strip," Berensen said. He turned in his chair and for the first time let the stern look on his face soften. "That's very good, for a greenhorn doctor. You related to the professor of neurosurgery at Northwestern?"

*Greenhorn* flashed across Susan's brain. She stared at the gray hair, then the face that registered years of experience and decided not to retort. "Pretty good for a female—and yes Doctor Arthur Benz is my father. After my year's service here in Appalachia, I'm going back to UK and do a residency under Doctor Wilson," she said, figuring it wasn't exactly a lie, maybe a hope, a new-found one.

"I understand you are taking him by helicopter to UK. I'll get films made of his CT so you can take them along," Berensen said.

Susan returned to the ER. Taswell grabbed her and took her to the room where Milton waited for transport to Lexington. "He raised his head, called for you, then fell back."

"By name?"

"Yeah. Susan, not Doctor Benz," Taswell said and proceeded to check Milton's blood pressure.

Susan approached the head of the cart, leaned over and softly said, "Milton, it's Susan."

Slight upturning of the corners of his mouth told her he heard. Deep inspirations followed, then the figure lay quietly. Taswell motioned to the doorway. Susan looked over her shoulder and spied Tooms.

He squinted at Milton and said, "They tell me the University helicopter will be here in forty minutes." He paused while Susan eased away from the cart and backpedaled toward him. "Come. We'll park your car at the van, and I'll take you by your apartment to get some things—I presume you will go with him to Lexington."

On the way to deposit her car behind the FBI van, Tooms told her he already had contacted the University security and told them about the stalker, adding he needed to remain in Harlan to supervise Home Security efforts at the coming demonstration. "If I thought cowboy's intentions were to do in Milton rather than disrupt his role in the marches, I'd assign an agent."

At her apartment Susan complied with Tooms's instructions and put on slacks with a white blouse, carrying her white coat over her arm. She stopped in the living room, put her overnight case on the coffee table in front of Tooms and asked, "Is this what you had in mind?"

He stood and while fishing in his pocket, said, "Perfect." He pinned a caduceus on the left lapel of her blouse. He turned the lapel over and pointed to a round object the size of her little fingertip. "That pulls off. Remove it with a counterclockwise motion."

Susan turned the soft, flesh-colored piece and pulled it off, watching as Tooms put a thick black belt around her waist. Next he held her left wrist, removed her wristwatch, stuck it in his pocket, and placed a larger one with a black wristband on her wrist. She watched with curiosity.

"Gently place the caduceus piece, hole end first, in your left ear," he said.

Susan obeyed, surveyed her new wristwatch. With both hands she examined the belt. Tooms watched silently until she looked into his eyes and said, "This must be some new FBI communication system. I know you are going to tell me how to use it."

Tooms grinned and pointed at the watch. "You pretend to wind the stem and move it forward. Go ahead." After Susan did that, he pushed one of the buttons on the side of his watch and said, "Doctor Benz, this is Tooms." Startled, Susan jerked her head back when she heard his words in her left ear.

With her overnight case in hand he went to the door. "Come, we don't have much time before the helicopter gets here."

On the way to the hospital Tooms told Susan that the belt had a built-in power source and served as receiver and transmitter. The belt relays messages from my watch or the van to the piece in your ear. If the piece is in place behind the caduceus, not in your ear, you will feel a vibration, imperceptible to others, in the belt. That's your signal to put the piece in your ear. Do it so no one knows what you did. To let us hear your voice or any sound around you, merely push the stem on your watch forward and talk normal."

"Simple. I understand, but you didn't tell me why."

"This cowboy seems to be bright, and should you encounter him, the first thing he would do is take away the palm pad—it's a common communication device. What I just gave you is bureau stuff."

"And?"

Tooms glanced at her, a sheepish look, as they pulled into the hospital parking lot. "Look, Susan. If I believed cowboy would go to Lexington—he'll know you and Milton went there, probably has been watching our every move—I would send Hank or Fetter, although hard to spare. Anyhow, you have a backup. Per my instructions with the palm pad, do not hesitate to use the earpiece and telewatch. Do it before you are convinced something is wrong or suspicious."

Susan listened intently, but watched two hospital orderlies load a stretcher with Milton onto the University helicopter. She grabbed her overnight case and climbed out. Before closing the door, she stuck her head in the car and said, "I'm nervous. I'll communicate through one device or the other regularly. Cowboy gives me the willies. You have more confidence in university security people than I. Bye."

The medical helicopter lifted off the hospital pad in Harlan with two pilots, a UK medical center nurse, Milton and Susan. In between adjusting the IV flow or taking Milton's vitals, the nurse conversed with Susan, asking her about Milton's problem, her medical experiences in the mountain town. Just before Lexington came into view, the nurse turned her head toward the stretcher. Milton's eyes were open, moving from the nurse and stopping on Susan's face. A weak grin moved across his face.

Susan slid to the head of the stretcher and leaned close, putting her face an inch from Milton's face. "You're on your way to the University of Kentucky Medical Center. This is their helicopter." The frown that replaced Milton's grin prompted her next comment. "You have a blood clot here." Susan pointed above her left ear. "That's why you have had headaches and passed out. They'll remove the clot through a tiny hole no bigger than this." She removed a pen from her blouse pocket and waved it before his eyes. "No bigger around than this. You'll feel normal by tomorrow morning and can..." She hesitated because his eyes opened wide and sparkled. His lips moved but the noise of the helicopter drowned out the message. He grinned, moving his lips. Her mind deciphered the words his lip movements made. Her heart jumped. Unbelieving, she put her ear to his mouth.

"I love you, Susan."

Tears clouded Susan's vision. She kissed an index finger and put it to Milton's lips. He smiled from ear to ear. Susan put her mouth to his ear and whispered. "I love you very much."

Those precious moments, his love expressed in words and in his eyes, carried her through the anxieties of the surgical preparations, the spell broken only by the warm welcome she received from Dr. Wilson. Waiting in the surgeons' lounge, Susan called Guthrie. Unable to book a flight that day from Chicago, Guthrie told her she was booked on the early bird special for Louisville and should arrive in Lexington late morning. Next she called her father. His answering service connected her. He was making evening rounds at Passavant Hospital, so briefly she told him about Milton and her stay of a few days in Lexington. Tooms called and asked about security. Holding her palm pad, she stepped to the door of the lounge and noted the security guard at the reception desk. Tooms was pleased, and before hanging up reminded her to be wary and not forget the back-up communication system. Fingering her belt, she reassured him.

Aroma of coffee registered in her brain. Susan jerked her head off her chest and peered into the smiling eyes of Horace Wilson. "They're working you too hard in Harlan, Susan," he said and handed her the cup of steamy brew.

She took the cup, sipped and said, "No one can work me too hard, Doctor Wilson. Things go okay in there?"

Wilson sat in a chair beside the couch. "Beautifully. The reverend's in recovery. Should go to surgical ICU in a half hour. Tomorrow he will feel better than he's felt in a long time."

Out the corner of her eye Susan saw the security guard leaning against the door jam. "Do you know about that?" She pointed to the man as she spoke.

"Security briefed me before you arrived. I've caught some of the news about Heiter, but why must they also protect you?"

Susan squirmed on the couch, searching for a way to tell Wilson her feelings. Finally, she said, "I'm Milton's doctor and whoever wants him to stop the demonstrations has been seen following me."

"That'd be Curewell—someone they hired. Yes?"

"Probably. He's such a well-liked pastor, I doubt he has any other enemy in the world."

Susan watched Wilson remove a key from his key ring. He handed her a key. "This key's for the faculty on-call suite, four rooms with a sitting area. A TV and a computer are for your use. Here's the code for internet use." Wilson gave her a slip of paper as he angled his head toward the door and added, "Sterling agrees the faculty suite is the best area for security."

Susan thanked Wilson and watched him disappear into the dressing room. The security guard escorted her to the cafeteria where Susan, under the guard's scrutiny, quieted the gnawing in her stomach with a ham and cheese sandwich chased by a glass of iced tea. By the time she had chatted with two former classmates who were in residency at the hospital, two hours had elapsed. She went to the surgical intensive care unit, smiled at a security guard sitting outside the ICU. Milton slept peacefully. Since he did not have any head dressing, Susan moved to the left side and when close saw two stitches that marked the location of the two drill holes. "Fantastic," she murmured as her peripheral vision caught a figure moving for the bed.

"His vitals are good, Doctor," a male nurse said.

"Has he been awake since he was moved in here?"

"Briefly."

"I'll spend the night in the faculty call room. Please call me if anything untoward happens," Susan told the man and headed for the hall.

"I'll do that and when he rouses, I'll tell him you were here checking," the man said.

Sterling followed Susan to the faculty on-call suite and pointing to a chair, said, "I'll be there throughout the night. The man replacing me at six in the morning is a tall redhead. "Sleep well, Doctor."

After Susan checked the other rooms and found them empty, she undressed, showered, and put on surgical scrubs for pajamas. She turned on the TV, surfed through channels until the ten o'clock news came on. After the woman spoke of the new breeding stables at Man-o-War farms, pictures of Harlan appeared on the screen behind the woman. The camera view zoomed from a distant view to a close-up, catching a crowd of people, several with placards. Fifty yards beyond the front row, contained by several state troopers, stood the parsonage, a corner of the Baxter Union Church visible to the left.

"The demonstration by NOW and Pro-choice folks started peacefully but state troopers had to be called in when several mountain folk dressed in their finest bib overalls came out of the woods from behind the home of the Reverend Heiter." The screen view changed, was filled with a man holding a placard that read, "Embryo research saves lives."

The camera panned to another placard. It read, "Heiter kills. Curewell heals."

In the background Susan heard chanting but couldn't decipher the words. The local anchor's face appeared in front of the parsonage scene as she said, "The gathering has been shouting for Reverend Heiter to come out and meet loved ones of people who have died because he held up cures embryo research might have produced." She pointed to the screen that showed a helicopter taking off from the Appalachian Regional Hospital. "We are told that the University Medical Center helicopter you see there transported the Reverend Heiter to Lexington. Folks here speculated that the reverend had a brain tumor. For the facts we have an interview with the neurosurgeon who operated on Heiter earlier this evening.

Susan moved to the edge of the chair when Wilson's face appeared on the screen. "Doctor Wilson, can you tell us what you found when you operated on Reverend Heiter?"

Wilson's cool professional countenance warmed with a suggestion of a grin. "Pastor Heiter had a subdural hematoma, one that came from a blow to his head he suffered in the bombing of his house over three weeks ago."

"And what is his condition at this time, sir?"

"He will recover rapidly. No aftereffects, 100 percent recovery," Wilson said.

The anchor's face reappeared on the screen and she said, "We are pleased that the Reverend Heiter will make a complete and rapid recovery. Unfortunately, he will not be able to lead tomorrow's march against his foe, Curewell Clinic."

Susan turned off the TV, peeked out the hall door and said goodnight to Sterling. She climbed in bed and suddenly Heiter's words struck her. "I want to get you close and personal with God." Susan climbed out of bed and kneeled at the bedside. Tears ran down her cheeks as she groped for a place to begin.

"God, you know what's in my heart, but I want to say my thoughts out loud. Forgive my sins and thank you for taking care of Milton today. Thank you for putting him in my life and for helping him love me." She glanced around the room, an eerie dirty yellow light reflecting off the far wall from a night-light. "I suppose you heard him say he loves me. You also know I love him. But I won't marry. He's nice to me. Men are nice so they can use me. They don't give up anything for women—never risk career, health, their own selfish ways for women. God, I don't deserve all I ask because of the mistakes I've made, but I need your help about our relationship. Another thing. We don't agree on when embryos and fetuses are beings. Teach me. Help me understand if I should be one with Milton, and what I should believe about the business of when a being exists. Milton thinks the being business is pretty important. I want so much to learn and have a faith as strong as Milton's. Amen."

Susan felt drained when she finally climbed under the covers. She fell asleep mumbling, "Milton, I love you more than anything in the world. I've asked God to tell me what I should do. And I asked Him to give me the answer about beings."

People were laughing, their conversation muted as it penetrated the door to her room. Susan bolted up in bed. Her hair was wet, stuck to the left side of her face. She eased out of bed and tiptoed to the door. With it ajar, she peered through the crack. The TV was on, but no one was in the sitting area. The doors to the other three rooms were wide open. Cautiously, she peered in one room after the other. No one, and each bed was made up. A thought jabbed her brain. She slowly opened the bathroom door. Empty, so she went in one stall and relieved herself. Sitting there she pondered the TV being on. Leaving the bathroom an idea struck her. Susan opened the hallway door. Sterling jumped out of the chair.

"Anything the matter, Doctor?" He stared at her hair.

"Has anybody come into the suite since I saw you last?"

"No m'am, and I've been wide awake the whole time," Sterling said. "Are you sure everything is okay?"

"I guess I forgot to turn off the TV before I retired. Everything's fine. Good night." She heard him say good night as she told herself, "I distinctly remember turning off the TV."

Susan shut the door and sat on the couch facing the TV. The clock on an end table told her it was two-ten in the morning. "You are a being from the moment the DNAs of the egg and sperm join." That demanding voice drew Susan's attention to the TV screen. "I am Bishop Jakes." An index finger of the black man in a white robe pointed at her. His other hand clutched a Bible. "I mean you," he shouted, causing Susan to stiffen on the edge of the couch. "It says so in these pages, yet you want scientific proof. No technology can do that. You don't have to under-stand—only believe." He thumped the Bible with his index fin-ger. "Jesus said those very words—they're in here. You want forgiveness, Susan?"

Susan jumped off the couch, moved close to the set, put her face close. She felt trickles of perspiration roll down her back. She wiped the matted hair off her face.

The man's face filled the screen. "Put your hand on the screen and say, 'I believe, God.'"

Susan put her hand on the screen and said, "I believe, God." She felt a shiver creep up her spine. The TV screen turned black and no sounds emanated from the set. Susan staggered to bed and fell asleep muttering, *I believe—I hear—I believe. God just answered one of my questions. What about Milton? Maybe He will show me that, too.*

# TEN

Quiet, so quiet and dark. Susan rolled on her back and tried to see objects in the windowless room. Once her feet hit the carpeted floor her brain fired up for the day, a hundred thoughts competing for attention. One cried out—"TV." She stopped in the doorway to the sitting room and stared at the dark screen of the TV. Like a bolt of lightning, the early morning scene flashed across her mind, and she pointed to the set, telling it, "I believe—I don't need to understand."

A quick shower helped her body catch up with her mind. After combing her short straight hair, she threw her pajamas, green surgical scrub top and bottom, on the bed. Fastening the belt given to her by Tooms caused a moment of introspection. Susan let her mind focus on security. She secured the strap to the watch from Tooms, put a white coat over the blouse, inspecting the caduceus as she did so. At the door to the hall she stopped, turned and retrieved her palm pad from her bag. When she opened the door and stepped into the hall, a young-looking security man jumped to his feet. He brushed back long reddish-brown hair.

"Good morning, Doctor Benz," he said, straightening his shirt collar. "I'm Merkle. Did you sleep well?"

"Thank you. I did except for the episode about two. Strange TV, Merkle."

"Sterling didn't tell me about any event. I'm to go to breakfast with you-–not eat, but be near."

Susan started for the hospital cafeteria, Merkle hovering close by. She said, "You can eat with me. It's okay."

The boyish smile was accompanied by a pink color, making the freckles on his cheeks light up. "I've eaten, but I'll sit and you can tell me about last night's episode."

"Can I bring you a cup of coffee?" Susan asked as she started through the line.

Merkle grinned and said, "Thanks. No cream or sugar."

Susan took a tray and put a glass of orange juice and an English muffin with two black coffees on it. She spied Merkle standing at a table. He pulled out a chair when she approached the table. "How long have you been a security guard?" she asked, trying not to reveal her conclusion that he looked too young to be in security.

"Two months. That's why I pull daytime duty. You are the first personal job I've had," he said.

*Thank goodness the cowboy isn't likely to travel here. This naive boy wouldn't discern a holy man from a gangster,* Susan thought while she finished the orange juice and started on the muffin.

"Tell me about the episode, Doctor."

"No big deal. Just that the TV woke me up around three, or two. I'm certain I turned it off before I went to bed. I asked Sterling if any faculty had come in the room."

"Probably a dream. Sterling told me he hadn't seen you since you retired for the night," Merkle said while he scanned the room, seeming to pause to study the occupants at each table.

After breakfast, Susan, with Merkle following behind, went to the surgical ICU. Milton sat up at a forty-five degree angle and was reading a newspaper. Susan reached the foot of the bed before he was aware of her presence. His spontaneous smile made her heart skip a beat. She glided to the side of the bed, leaned over and pecked his cheek. His gray-blue eyes sparkled. She felt a warm rush engulf her.

"You look better than ever," she said.

"I feel wonderful, but Doctor Wilson said I have to stay until Monday." Milton grabbed her hand and held tightly. "How blessed I am to have such a caring doctor, one..." He stopped with his mouth half open. He searched her eyes, his talking to her.

Susan felt her face grow warm. "One what?"

He broke into his magnificent grin and said, "One I love. The one who has taken care of my physical ailments, one who brings sunshine into my life."

Tears flowed from Susan's eyes, blurring a subtle grin that turned to an ear-to-ear grin. She put her right hand over his hand and said, "My pastor, the one who takes care of my soul, stirs my being." She paused, for that word brought a flashback. "I had a dream last night and God answered my bedtime prayer. He answered one of my questions. He told me I didn't need to understand, only believe. Know what? I believe embryos and fetuses are beings from the moment two DNAs join."

Milton's mouth flew open, his eyes doubled in size. "Sounds more like a visitation than a dream, Susan." Milton sat upright, put his hand on her hands. His countenance turned serious. "You said He answered one of your questions. What was the other question?"

"I asked Him to..." The rest of the thought stuck in her mind and she ruminated silently, *I shouldn't have said that.* Her eyes dropped to their hands. She shuffled her feet as she mumbled, "It must wait for His answer—His help, Milton."

A warm hand under Susan's chin raised her head. Piercing eyes reached her soul. His eyebrows nearly touched each other. "I'm not good enough for you, but I believe God has put us through so much together so we can pursue him as a married couple." His face transformed into a warm, fuzzy blur when he added, "That was a lovesick preacher's proposal. I know you don't think you should marry. Ask God what you should do. He's listening."

Susan wrenched her hands free, threw them across her chest, stiffened, and said, "That was my other question. I asked God to remove my doubts about marriage—my fears about marrying." She leaned back and put her hands on her hips, having heard footsteps approaching the alcove. Susan wiped tears from her cheeks and said, "I believe—I believe He will give me a sign."

"Sometimes when we ask for a sign, we may not like the cost, Susan. But God will answer you whether..."

A white figure burst into the room. "Doctor, I hate to ask you to leave, but we have to get the reverend ready for transfer. He's being moved to third floor, an end room so they"—the nurse pointed to a security guard standing outside the alcove—"can keep watch over him. And you'll be able to visit as long as you wish."

Susan told Milton she would see him after lunch, probably bring Guthrie. She went to the faculty suite, sat on the couch and dialed her father's number on the palm pad. His answering service responded and told Susan he was signed out to an associate for the day. Next, Susan called his apartment. The answering machine said to leave a message, so Susan said hi, gave the time of her message and said she was in Lexington where Milton Heiter was recovering from surgery for a subdural hematoma. Remembering that the demonstration in Harlan was to begin mid-morning, she turned on the TV to catch the eleven o'clock news. The view of Broadway in Harlan appeared on the screen. No cars, the street was jammed with people, some carrying placards. While the announcer described the participants in the march that began in Baxter at Reverend Heiter's house, the view changed. Police restrained a crowd some fifty yards from the Curewell Clinic.

"The leader of the group, the Reverend Heiter, is not present," a male voice said as the camera zoomed on faces in the front row of the crowd. Susan squinted at the screen when Jethroe's face came into focus. A woman holding a microphone stood beside him. The announcer said, "We have Katherine Hardin amongst the demonstrators. Katherine, who do you have there?"

"Michael, this is Jethroe Caulder. He is Reverend Heiter's assistant. In Heiter's absence Jethroe led the march from the church in Baxter to the Curewell Clinic, which you see behind me." The camera moved from her face to Jethroe's as she spoke to him. "Mr. Caulder, have you heard how Pastor Heiter is doing this morning?"

Tension registered on Jethroe's face. His eyes flitted from side to side. He stammered momentarily and then gushed, "Shucks m'am, no need callin' me Mister. I..."

A smooth, low voice interrupted him. "Okay Jethroe. I like that name. Is it your pa's name?"

That approach seemed to relax Jethroe. He smiled weakly. "Named after my grandpa Jethroe." He giggled, then put on a serious face and said, "He were a fine hooch maker. I don't do nuthin' like that. Ain't never had a poke. Agent Tooms told me this mornin' that Pastor Heiter is doin' fine. May come home Monday, preach the next Sunday."

"Jethroe, I understand you led the marchers in prayer at the church before they started for here," the woman said.

"Not me. 'Twas a bunch of exhortative prayin'," Jethroe said.

The woman's next question was drowned out by yelling and loud cries. The camera shifted to her right where a fracas was underway. Two opposing groups were shoving and yelling indecipherably. The camera switched to the announcer, who said, "It seems we have lost our audio with Katherine Hardin. What you saw briefly was a confrontation between the forces brought to the clinic by this Jethroe who it appears is the leader, although an unlikely one, in Heiter's absence. Maxwell Tooms, the FBI agent in charge in Harlan, told us he had called regional Home Security to come oversee the weekend demonstrations. Expectations have mounted as the week progressed because members of several national organizations have arrived. We will keep you updated on events in Harlan, but right now we have a news release we received from Atlanta." Susan watched while a reporter in Atlanta told of a demonstration against the Curewell Clinic in Atlanta. Pictures of a wild melee appeared behind the reporter. The ringing of the phone on the end table captured Susan's attention. She hit the mute button and removed the receiver from its base.

"This is Doctor Benz," she said.

"Hi Susan. Horace Wilson here. Your pastor friend is getting along well. As we speak he is being moved to a private room, so you can visit more. He told me his twin sister is on her way here. If she wishes to speak with me, don't hesitate to give her my cell phone number."

After a brief conversation about Susan taking a spot in the neurosurgery residency, Susan, followed by Merkle, ate a light lunch, a cheese and ham sandwich with a glass of milk, and went to the third floor. The security guard sitting by a door at the end of the hall told Susan where Milton had been moved. She identified herself and politely thanked the receptionist behind the counter for the room number. She entered the room. Milton was watching television. The same announcer was giving an update of events in Harlan. She eased to the bedside and took Milton's hand.

He smiled, pointed to the TV and said, "Look, Susan. When a ruckus started, Jethroe herded the mountain folks, those who had gathered at the church, back to Baxter." He shifted his gaze from the screen to her face. "Have you seen the earlier news about the confrontations?"

"Just the beginning, and then they switched to Atlanta where that Curewell Clinic was having a similar, maybe wilder demonstration. I've not seen anything for the past couple hours."

"Half hour ago, they showed a live take of a similar demonstration at the Curewell Clinic in Los Angeles. Some arrests made there." Milton held the remote, turned off the TV and surveyed Susan, his eyes resting on her wrist. "You have a new watch."

Susan looked over her shoulder, scooted a chair close to the bed and softly said, "Tooms gave it to me, and this belt." Milton leaned to the side of the bed and stared at the belt. "Backup security in case my palm pad doesn't function." She held the caduceus with one hand and removed the earpiece with the other. She twirled it between thumb and forefinger and said, "This is the receiving part, the watch the broadcast, and the belt is the transmitter and power source."

Milton frowned. "If Tooms was so concerned I would think he might have sent an agent here." Milton grabbed her hand and held it while he took the earpiece and examined it.

"Just cautious," Susan said, and took the earpiece from him. He held her hand and smiled, so she stuck the earpiece in her left ear. "Doctor Wison has virtually offered me a spot in his neurosurgery program beginning next July one. Do you think that offer to come here from Harlan was God's answer?"

Milton beamed and said, "The offer answered questions you may have had about your career, not about us." Voices outside the room drew his attention. Susan turned in time to see a woman who appeared to be Milton's age burst into the room. She looked past Susan, strode to the other side of the bed and proceeded to plant a kiss on Milton's cheek. Milton threw his arms about her neck, pulled away a bit and said, "Guthrie, you look too pretty to be a scientist." He turned his head toward Susan, winked and said, "Meet Susan, Sis. Susan, this is Guthrie Heiter Vorland."

Guthrie straightened at the bedside as Susan pushed out of the chair and extended a hand across the bed. Bizarre. Guthrie pushed Susan's hand away, dashed around the bed and stepped to within three feet. Slowly with a cool look Guthrie let her eyes dissect every inch of Susan's figure, beginning with her face and stopping at her feet.

Uncertain as to the cool scrutiny, Susan extended a hand and said, "We've talked. I'm Susan Benz, Guthrie."

Again Guthrie pushed the hand away, stepped close and suddenly hugged Susan. When she released her, Guthrie's face was all smile, her eyes warm and watery. She said, "Perfect. You are perfect for the second most important man in my life. Since you came into his life, Milton has changed for the better." Guthrie turned to Milton. "It took surgery to wake you up."

Guthrie grabbed a chair from a corner and pulled it beside the bed opposite Susan. Susan listened while Milton described his recovery and then asked Susan to tell Guthrie about the events in Harlan, Atlanta, and Los Angeles.

"All this turmoil because you clergy types believe an embryo is a being," Guthrie said with a tone that had changed from warm and friendly to brisk and challenging. Her gaze bounced from Milton to Susan.

Susan felt uncomfortable under the stern gaze. She looked at Milton. His presence had changed as well. She recognized his professional demeanor, except, when he glanced at her, he sent his message of caring. Susan spoke to Guthrie, putting on a demure grin. "Some scientists—I'm one—believe like preachers that when two DNAs join, a being exists, Guthrie."

"Well, well. Love and emotions cloud your scientific mind, Doctor?" Guthrie hissed at Susan.

Milton waved a hand at Susan. "And does the smell of money cloud your Christian upbringing, Sis? If Helpgene makes big discoveries from stem cells, you will undoubtedly get a big raise."

Susan watched the sparks fly between brother and sister when Guthrie retorted. "Milt…"

"Don't call me Milt. Never."

Guthrie looked across the bed at Susan and said, "He has bad memories when he is called Milt because that's what his ex-wife called him." She looked across at Milton and said, "Helpgene does genetic therapy research. We do not use embryos for stem cells."

"Same difference, Guthrie." Milton screwed up his face at her.

Guthrie turned her gaze on Susan again and sneered, "I'll explain to you, Susan. Maybe you can get it through his thick skull. Helpgene has been doing research on genetic engineering since 1971. We were one of the first companies. Our focus has been on gene therapy." She threw a quick glance at Milton and continued, "Our focus has been in two general areas; one is work with genes that produce a depressed product. Insulin deficiency is a good example. Now we can introduce into a diabetic a gene that will produce insulin, so the patient doesn't have to take shots or, if lucky, a pill to make up for deficient production by their pancreas. The other type gene therapy uses a gene that produces a substance called antisense because it elaborates a product that blocks a harmful product. Rheumatoid arthritis is an example of that type disease."

"But if you alter the genetic make up of the patient you will be altering all the kids from that person," Milton said.

"Wrong. We use somatic cells for gene therapy. They only alter gene function of that person. If germ cells are used in gene therapy the genetic change is passed on to offspring. The danger with that is the problem with gene expression in future generations. I'll bet Susan knows why."

When Milton didn't say anything, just stared expectantly at her, Susan said, "Sure. Most genetic diseases involve more than one gene defect. Genetic expression and signals that regulate gene function are huge problems." She smiled at Guthrie.

"Good. And Helpgene spends most of its resources on the one aspect of genetic engineering that has held back significant progress. Proteinomics, the study of proteins that serve as signals controlling gene function and expression. That is why we disagree with companies such as Curewell. They are using up," she paused to grin at Milton and added, "they are killing embryos before they have an understanding of the signals involved. Good researchers don't jump ahead of the next logical, crucial step in unraveling scientific mysteries."

"If you're in it for big bucks, you jump over several steps, Guthrie," Milton said.

"Curewell does. We aren't in the big money game at Helpgene, Brother."

"What are the important steps in gene therapy?" Susan relaxed. The atmosphere had changed from combative to discussion.

"The first step, identify the gene associated with the disease, or as you stated, the genes for most genetic diseases. The second step is finding a good transport or delivery system. A vector carries the gene safely to the target. One of the earliest was a virus called a filovirus. It carried the gene used to treat cystic fibrosis because filovirus is attracted to and penetrates the lining of the human airway. Sometimes chemicals are used. But finding a good vector has been the stumbling block that has slowed progress over the last ten years. I don't think the delay has been so bad because the third step, controlling gene expression in altered cells, has been difficult."

"And a nightmare for clinics like Curewell who have used embryonic stem cells to treat genetic diseases. I remember the earliest clinical trials where they used such cells and couldn't control the gene function," Susan said.

"Correct. One twenty-year-old died, and some patients with Parkinson's disease ended up with uncontrollable twitches because the output by the implanted cells couldn't be controlled," Guthrie said.

"So if Helpgene doesn't use embryos, why don't you believe embryos are beings? You don't have to defend your company or your research," Milton said.

"That's not why I feel the way I do, Brother. I just don't know. I don't have any scientific evidence to help me decide or understand," Guthrie said.

"Scientists have no evidence about beings, when they begin and when they depart the body. Same for the soul, Guthrie." Susan threw a smile at Milton. "Last night a TV preacher woke me up. The twenty-ninth chapter of Isaiah, the fourteenth verse, says God withholds understanding from us." She saw Milton grab a Bible off his bedside stand.

"Isaiah is telling the Israelis about their hypocrisy. Their situation was very similar to ours today. In verse thirteen he tells them that God sees them draw close with their mouths and with their lips they honor Him, but they have removed their hearts far from Him and their fear of Him is taught by precept of men. Susan is correct. Let me read the fourteenth verse.

*Therefore, behold, I will proceed to do a marvelous work*
*among these people, even a marvelous work and a wonder:*

*for the wisdom of their wise men shall perish, and the under-
standing of their prudent men shall perish."*

Guthrie scooted up on her chair. "That scripture speaks to my
scientist friends who think because they make a discovery, God
means it to be used without considering moral or ethical implica-
tions. That's why I am happy in my work at Helpgene. Also, the
other scientists jump into treatments, seeming to give little consideration to things, such as the effect of their untested therapy on
long-term results, the effect on gene pool, genetic flux, and rights of
future offspring, to name a few."

Milton's mouth stood open. He nodded his head slowly while
he waved a nurse in. She stood at the end of the bed and said, "I
hate to interrupt such an erudite conversation but you must rest,
Reverend Heiter."

"I'll let them go after I read what God said will happen to the
Curewells." He picked up the Bible again and continued to read
from Isaiah:

*"Woe unto them that seek deep to hide their counsel from
the Lord, and their works are in the dark, and they say, Who
seeth us? and knoweth us?"*

Susan pushed back her chair and followed Guthrie to the door.
They said goodbye to Milton. Guthrie picked up her suitcase resting
against the security guard's chair and followed Susan to the faculty
suite.

After Guthrie showered and changed into more casual attire,
Susan took her to the cafeteria. Merkle followed but declined her
invitation to join them for dinner. The two women reviewed the
afternoon's conversation with Milton, and Susan told Guthrie
about the previous night's TV episode and how she came to realize
that as a Christian scientist and doctor she needed only to believe
that embryos are beings, not necessarily understand from scientific
evidence.

Throughout dinner Guthrie seemed to grow more withdrawn and whenever Susan changed the subject to her love for Milton and their talk of marriage, Guthrie changed the subject back to the afternoon's discussion. The reason surfaced after they returned from a brief after-dinner meeting in Milton's room.

"Have I offended you? Am I not acceptable to twin sister as a close friend for Milton? He wants to marry me."

Guthrie looked about the room and let her eyes rest on the computer. "Are you permitted to use that for internet access?"

"Yes," Susan replied.

Guthrie moved over to the computer and pulled a chair to the desk, at the same time motioning for Susan to pull up a chair that stood beside the door. The screen lit up. Susan punched in the code Wilson had given her and Guthrie hit the Internet Explorer icon. Next in the search box she typed helpgenearchiv@indust.org.

Guthrie hesitated, turned toward Susan. "You have not offended me. I carried on with Milton this afternoon because I didn't know how to speak to a problem."

"Problem?"

"Marriage between you and Milton."

The room grew hot. Susan searched Guthrie's eyes and said, "You don't think—because of my past—that I'm good enough to be his wife." She felt anger rise to the top of her head.

Guthrie reached over and clasped Susan's shoulder. The warmth her eyes exuded disarmed Susan. "To the contrary. You would be perfect for him. And he loves you deeply. But what I will show you will dampen your love, Sister."

While Guthrie faced the screen and punched in more code, Susan said, "Sister." She watched as Guthrie pointed to the screen.

"Helpgene has a record in their archives of the first ten years of embryos produced by their lab. There," she pointed to the fourth name on the screen, "see, that's our mom and dad's entry. Note three embryos were obtained from in-vitro fertilization. She highlighted the name Heiter and punched the mouse. The next screen stunned Susan as she read out loud, "Embryo one and two implanted into uterus of Mrs. Heiter on November 7, 1979.

Embryo three frozen and sold to Northwestern University Fertility Clinic for Professor Arthur Benz."

Tears rolled down Susan's cheeks. She felt nauseated and leaned her head on Guthrie's shoulder. Guthrie pointed to an asterisk under the last line and read, "Embryo implanted in surrogate June 14, 1981." She turned so Susan's face buried in her chest.

From the depth of her soul Susan let sob after sob rack her body. Guthrie lifted her head and held it so their eyes locked on each other's. The stream of tears continued to run down Susan's cheeks, onto her lips, down her chin, down her neck. The salty taste seemed like salt in a wound. "Oh, Guthrie," she wailed. Susan looked toward the ceiling and continued, "God just answered my second request—should I marry Milton?"

For an hour before Guthrie turned off Susan's bedroom light and went to her room, they talked as if two sisters, Susan lamenting that she didn't love Milton as a brother, Guthrie attempting a conciliatory thought that the two of them were sisters and could still look after Milton.

Sleep wouldn't come, only more tears and an incessant trembling. Susan's soul whimpered while her mind searched every nook and cranny for the road to peace. Finally, Milton's words raced across her brain. She crawled from under the covers and kneeled beside the bed. "Oh God, I am wounded to my very soul. I found a man to love as you meant me to love, a man who led me to you, to help heal my sick soul. Why, oh God, must I suffer such a trick? Help me in my hour of torment. Milton said I might not like the cost." Susan crawled in bed but lightning flashed before her eyes. "Oh no. God, forgive my selfishness. Milton loves me so and has been tortured once before by love. I don't deserve your mercy but he does. Comfort him and help him through this, please."

Susan squeezed her eyelids tightly together. Still, images of Milton paraded across the backs of her eyelids. The images didn't blur when tears flooded her eye sockets and wet her surgical scrub top. "Milton, I love you more than life. I can't pursue my new relationship with God as your wife. He wants me to dedicate my life to helping neurosurgical patients."

# ELEVEN

**Milton** Heiter opened his left eye and then slowly the right one. He smiled at the hundreds of dots on the false ceiling of the refurbished private room. "Each of those represents days I will spend with Susan, because I know what God will say. Imagine, Milton, a neurosurgeon for a wife. Won't parishioners have a feast with that," he told the remote and hit the nurse call button.

He enjoyed the dance that the sun's rays were having on the window drapes. He threw the covers off and dangled his legs over the edge of the bed when a voice came over the intercom. "May I help you, Reverend?"

"No, but may I get out of bed? I feel like a new man."

"Absolutely not," came the stern reply. "You stay in bed. I'm coming with your breakfast." *Sunday morning and I'm stuck in here. I should be holding church service*, he mused.

A nursing assistant marched through the doorway, food tray in hand. She pushed the bed table over his legs and sat the tray on it and left. He had demolished the eggs and sausage when Wilson entered.

"Feeling pretty chipper, eh? Well, I'll let you up in a chair this morning. Doctor Benz can walk you around the ward this afternoon, and if that goes well, I'll release you in the morning," Wilson said while he made a note on Milton's chart.

"Sounds good to me. What restrictions?"

"No straining. No lifting or running. Don't take any medicines unless Doctor Benz says it's okay. We don't want any bleeding in your noggin. She can take the two stitches out on Friday."

Milton waited for two minutes after Wilson left and yelled, "Yahoo!" He picked up the phone and dialed the faculty on-call room. No answer. They're probably at church, he reasoned, leaned back and flipped the TV channels until he found a church service.

Shortly after lunch, Guthrie slinked into the room. Her walk sounded the alert. Milton waited. He kept both eyes glued to the door. No Susan. Guthrie jabbered about the lovely day, how well he looked, and what the nurse told her about his progress and discharge in the morning. Motor mouth, he thought until the continuous senseless monologue by Guthrie struck his suspicious vein.

"Where is she, Guthrie? She's safe, isn't she?"

Guthrie came over, flashed a folded paper before his eyes. He took it and read it quickly. The message forced him to read it again, slowly.

> Milt:
> I can't be near you now. It'd drive me crazy. I am going ahead to Harlan with my father. I need time to sort through this. Guthrie has a paper that will explain.
>
> Susan

Milton read it again, and again and again, each time recovering a bit from the shock and growing suspicions. Guthrie gave him a paper and said, "Susan is our sister. She's the third embryo from Mom and Dad's in-vitro fertilization."

He hardly noticed the tears running down his cheeks but he had to wipe his eyes with the sheet so he could read the paper. He read it twice, dropped it and stared at Guthrie. She sat on the edge of the bed beside him and put her arm around him.

"Maybe, the love you two felt was sibling love."

Studying the printout he said, "Well, I think God gave Susan the answer to her second question. And an answer for me. I think God wants me to devote my life to Him and His way—unencumbered by a woman. Funny, He did that once before. I was too stiff-necked to listen."

A nurse came and helped Milton sit in a chair. Guthrie pulled a chair from the corner close to his and started jabbering about their growing-up years. Milton didn't hear a word. His soul ached. The room looked like a dungeon, the sun didn't shine anymore.

Without thinking he pushed out of the chair and snatched the two pieces of paper off the bedtable. He paced around the room. Guthrie stopped her chatter and watched. He stopped in front of her and, waving the papers said, "Are you sure she didn't tell you something else? Look at this note from her," he threw the note on Guthrie's lap. "She must be mad at me. She knows I hate being called Milt. What did she say when she gave you the note?"

"When I came back from the cafeteria she was gone. That note was on the coffee table. That red-headed security guard said her father showed up and..."

"You're sure. Maybe Susan was alerting me by addressing me as Milt. Did this greenhorn guard get proof, some ID, that the man was her father?"

"Come on. I know about this stalker, the cowboy. Merkle, that's the guard's name. He said the man was very professorial, acknowledged he knew about the reason for your and Susan's protection. He proceeded to show ID from Northwestern Medical Center with his picture on the laminated card that read 'Professor Arthur Benz.' Merkle said Susan shook her head yes when she came to the door and the man stood before her. He said she reacted like any daughter who had a surprise visit by a famous father."

"Hey, guard!" Milton yelled toward the doorway.

A graying, round-faced man entered and said, "What can I do for you, Reverend?"

"Were you aware that Doctor Benz left with a man that was supposedly her father?"

The guard jumped to the bedside stand and grabbed the phone. He picked up the receiver. "Yeah, this is Teller. Is Merkle still on duty?" He nodded his head up and down. "Seven-eight-one. Thanks." Milton watched the man remove a cell phone from his belt and punch in three numbers. "Merkle, Teller here. I just learned that Doctor Benz left with her father. Tell me how you identified him." Teller listened, shaking his head intermittently. "Sounds legit, Merkle. When you put the note on the coffee table for Doctor Vorland, did you look around the suite? See anything unusual, any-thing suspicious?" Teller listened briefly. He turned toward Guthrie and asked, "Do you have a black palm pad, perchance?"

Guthrie removed a brown rectangular object from her purse and showed the object with buttons on the bottom half and a small screen on the top half. "Tell me the kind of palm pad." He began to frown and said, "Okay, bring it over here. The preacher can ID it."

Teller quizzed Guthrie about the time she went to eat break-fast, why Susan didn't go, and if she saw anybody wearing cowboy boots and a huge belt with a green cattle skull and horns on the buckle. *At least this guy seems to be on the ball,* Milton concluded.

Merkle entered the room and handed a black object to Teller. "This Doctor Benz's palm pad, Reverend Heiter?" he asked and handed it to Milton.

Milton opened it and immediately recognized it. "Yes, it is Susan's."

"Where did you find this, Merkle?" Teller reached for the pad but Milton hugged it to his chest.

"I found it alongside her bed. The room was a bit of a mess. The doctor must have a maid in Harlan," Merkle said.

Guthrie said, "That's strange. When I stood in the doorway to her room she was making the bed, explaining to me she was too upset to eat. The room was tidy. In fact, the bed was made and she was fluffing the pillows as I departed."

Milton began to put together his suspicions as Teller quizzed Merkle about the ID of Professor Benz. He opened Susan's palm pad and pushed the red button. A face appeared on the screen and a voice, "Yes, Doctor Benz."

Teller turned silent and eyes of the three people stared at Milton. "This is Milton Heiter. Doctor Benz forgot this when she left here to return to Harlan with her father this morning. Does Tooms know she's on her way back?"

"I don't think so. Push the pound sign three times in rapid succession and you'll get Tooms. And when you talk, position the screen in front of your face."

"One more thing. Does the pad have frequently dialed numbers stored under a code?"

"Yes, Reverend, star and one-two. Want me to get Tooms for you? He must know about this."

"I'll get him after one tell tale call. Bye." Milton ended the conversation and punched star one-two. The others in the room stared.

"This is Doctor Arthur Benz," a smooth professional sounding voice rolled out of the pad. Suddenly fright trapped Milton's tongue. *I mustn't alarm him until I know more*, he thought. He held the pad in front of his face. "Hi, Doctor Benz. This is Milton Heiter. Nice to meet you."

"Now preachers have these modern telephones. Amazing," Benz said.

"I wanted to show you that I am recovered, thanks to the skills of your daughter."

"Put her on. She tried to reach me yesterday, but I was out on my sailboat, signed out to a colleague."

That remark opened the door to the reason for his call: Where was the professor now? "Can you see the sailboats from your seventeenth-floor apartment?"

A view of blue water with small ant-like sailboats appeared on the screen. "You can't make them out very well from up here but they're having a good day on ole mother Lake Michigan."

Milton sat, buying time for his next tack. "Sorry, today's the first I've been out of bed." He put the pad screen in front of Guthrie and said, "Meet my twin sister, Doctor Guthrie Vorland from Aurora. Susan went back to Harlan this morning. I'm going back in the morning. I just wanted to thank you personally for having a neat daughter."

Milton turned the screen toward his face as Benz said, "Nice family. Susan has told me all about you and your family. When your two DNAs meet they'll produce some great grandkids for me, Reverend."

Tears filled Milton's eyes. He moved the pad further from his face so his features would be blurry. "The life of a preacher's wife can be pretty confining, Doctor," he said.

"Well, being married to a neurosurgeon isn't a bed of roses. But love is a great bond. Goodbye, Milton. I hope to see you in person soon."

"Goodbye, Professor," Milton said and closed the pad.

Guthrie patted his arm and said, "You are so brave."

"So, if Professor Benz is in Chicago, who was that here this morning?" Merkle asked, his face saying he knew the answer.

"Cowboy," Milton answered and punched the pound sign rapidly three times. He watched Teller thump on Merkle's chest. Guthrie removed a pad from her pursue.

"Hi Susan. What's up?" Maxwell Tooms's face appeared on the screen.

Milton held it before his face and began to tell Tooms about the man who posed as Susan's father and the abandoned palm pad he was using. When he told Tooms he had just talked to Susan's father in Chicago, Tooms let out a string of Herculean oaths.

Tooms frowned and said, "Milton, good work. Let me get back to you. Earlier, around breakfast time, we got an emergency communication from that palm pad, but no voice, only a man's face. Let me check that. I'll call you."

Closing the palm pad, Milton went to the bed and pushed the nurse call button. "Yes, Reverend," came over the intercom.

"An emergency has arisen in Harlan. Would you please get hold of Doctor Wilson and tell him I need to be discharged today—soon! The FBI will send a helicopter for me so it won't be stressful." *I'm sure Tooms will do that,* he thought while he listened.

The voice broke into his thoughts. "I will try, Reverend."

Waiting impatiently, Milton paced around the bed, a thousand thoughts pounding in his brain. Merkle and Teller stood in the doorway. Guthrie, notepad in hand, hovered at the head of the bed. Ringing chopped off Milton's planning, a scheme to rescue Susan.

"For you, Milton. It's Doctor Wilson," Guthrie said, holding the phone toward him.

Milton took the receiver from Guthrie and put it to his ear, saying a silent prayer, *Please, Lord.* "Milton, I heard someone abducted Susan. And you want to go to Harlan," Wilson spoke tersely.

"Yes, and I'm the only one that can barter for her release. I must go."

"If you can travel by helicopter, go. Just let others do for you. No lifting or bending over—squat. No straining or running. Take it slow and easy. I've given the verbal order. You may go any time. Do a good job. I want Susan to be my resident next July. God's speed, Milton."

The palm pad buzzed. Milton opened it and stared at Tooms's face. "Milton, I'm going to put a man's image on the screen. Tell me if you recognize him."

"Oh, no," Milton mumbled while he studied the face on the pad screen. He tilted the pad, moved it closer and then further away until the features were in perfect focus.

Tooms said, "I didn't catch that, Milton."

Milton put the pad in front of his face. "That's Joseph Elbergard. Two years ago I counseled his wife to leave him. For months she would come to me all beat up. She went to her parents in Ohio."

"Great. We'll get background on him," Tooms said.

"Max, I've been released. Can come to Harlan, if I can travel by helicopter. Could…"

"I'll send one immediately. Susan's father is flying down as we speak—a private jet. Try to rest 'til I see you. We'll need you to be perfectly alert when you get here."

Tooms's face disappeared from the screen. Guthrie went to collect her things from the faculty on-call suite. A nurse brought Milton his clothes. *Sunday, a day of rest*, Milton muttered while he slipped on his shirt. Of course I'll rest, Tooms. No worry. Some maniac has my newly found sister and…. That repressed thought tied his brain in knots. Gently, he shook his head, stuffed the shirt in his trousers, started to tie his shoes, but straightened. He sat in a chair and raised one foot after the other, tying the laces without bending down. He reached up to the bed table and clutched the Bible to his chest and spoke out loud, "Lord, God, my protector, my savior. Like my sister Susan, I don't understand. But I believe. I believe I can do all things through Christ which strengthens me. Guide me, use me to free Susan. Jesus, through you all things are possible. May no one get hurt during today's events, not even Joseph Elbergard. Lord, I pray for his forgiveness if I wronged him in trying to protect his wife. Please, dear God, be with us this day."

Heavy, rhythmic beating of the helicopter blades seemed to be a soporific for Milton. On takeoff from the hospital helipad,

Guthrie had started to chatter, her usual nervous mode, but some-time shortly after getting airborne he heard only helicopter sounds. An interlude of silence when the helicopter sat down in the park-ing lot of his church in Baxter was soon replaced by people sounds and the metallic sound of the helicopter door opening.

A hand squeezed his arm. "We're here, Milton," Guthrie said.

Milton opened his eyes and blinked at the bright afternoon sun. Guthrie stepped over him and the pilot helped her to the gravel. Milton took in the view to his right. He smiled. The church and the parsonage warmed a spot deep inside. A black car pulled into the lot. He watched Tooms hustle to the helicopter. He eased to the door.

"Here, Milton, let me give you a hand," Tooms said. Once Milton stood on the gravel, Tooms looked him up and down. No smile but a gentle, almost tender countenance on his face. "Come inside. We have to move quickly and precisely."

In spite of the consternation those words evoked, Milton felt a flicker of exhilaration when he mounted the steps to the back porch. *I'm home, Lord. Thank you. And I owe that to Susan. Oh, Susan.* Tooms stopped his mental gyrations. He had followed Tooms into the living room. "Milton, this is Professor Benz."

The tall, lean man appeared to be about sixty and looked much more vibrant than he had on the palm pad screen. His eyes danced as he extended a hand to Milton. The grasp was almost hard and his eyes bore through Milton. He maintained the grip when Milton tried to remove his hand. "Milton, you are not bad looking for a preacher." He looked over Milton's shoulder and added, "And this would be your twin sister Guthrie. A geneticist."

Tooms stepped over to the TV, stuck his hand behind it and turned it on. Milton nodded, for he knew the central command would be the next image on the screen. "Susan doesn't look like Susan or me, although she has a suggestion of resemblance to our mother when she was younger," Milton said and pulled his hand out of Benz's grasp.

Guthrie seemed deep in thought but smiled and nodded at Benz. "Susan is a sweet girl. One thing. I work at Helpgene and accessed their archives. It said Northwestern's Fertility Clinic bought Ma and Pa's third embryo and implanted it in a surrogate almost two years after Milton and I were implanted in mother's uterus. But Susan says she is twenty-six—a two-year discrepancy."

Milton watched the frown grow on Benz's face. Tooms called for the three to come look at the TV screen. A small white bungalow occupied the right half of the screen. The FBI van was to the right, parked on the street, about one hundred yards from the house. Tooms directed a finger at the house. "Behind the drawn curtains of the front window, your nemesis holds Susan." He paused while two men entered from the back and put a pile of clothing on the couch. "He has a rifle in his left hand. He keeps Susan at his right side, continually threatens her, and demands to see you, Milton."

"How can you be so sure of these things, Max?" Milton watched Tooms search the pile of clothes and wave a pair of white long underwear at him.

Tooms pushed a button on his watch and said, "Boys, put the front room surveillance view on the screen." The images were two silhouettes, gray but easily identified as a female positioned between the window and the partial outline of a male silhouette. Before Milton could ask how that worked, Tooms said, "From the Afghanistan war. Computer takes the heat sensor and laser waves and creates the images. Easy through cloth, not as sharp through, say the wooden siding, but still helpful." He walked toward the bedroom with the long johns. "Come, you need to put these on if you still want to talk to this sicko."

"Does Elbergard know Susan is my sister, not my girlfriend?" Milton said but was stopped at the door to the bedroom by a firm hand on his shoulder.

He turned and looked at the puzzled face of Benz. "What are you talking…" The man's face changed to a grin. "I get it. The third embryo. I did purchase that embryo, and it was implanted some twenty months after the first two, you and Guthrie. But the surrogate lost it. Two years later Northwestern purchased another, scientist father and beauty queen mother. The surrogate didn't lose that embryo and that one grew up to be the Susan Benz you know."

Astounded, Milton felt an urge to hug the man, but Guthrie threw herself at him and held him hard, saying, "Oh Milton, oh Milton."

"Guthrie, that message that Susan received and I saw this morning—the one that told us she is our sister wasn't from God. He doesn't send incorrect signs or answers. Thanks, Doctor Benz. Now I can ask for your daughter's hand," Milton said and, grabbing the long underwear from Tooms, went into his bedroom.

Through the closed door Benz yelled, "Guthrie told me of Susan's prayer—a request for help from God. She hasn't received the answer to her second request for help, some indication of what her relationship to you should be."

Milton stepped out of the bedroom sporting only the long underwear and Guthrie grinned and said, "Neat preacher's garb, Brother. What about Susan's second request of God?"

Tooms gave Milton a pair of dark blue trousers and then a thick white summer shirt. Milton felt them and looked at Tooms. "I figure the longies are bullet proof. Are these? They seem too light to be bullet proof." He looked at Guthrie first and then Professor Benz and said, "I don't know. But He is unfailing. He'll tell her."

Tooms motioned to Benz and said, "With both the shirt and longies, a bullet from a high-powered rifle won't make a scratch."

When that comment registered in Milton's brain, a burst of adrenalin sped up his pulse rate and fear washed over him. He reminded himself that he was doing this to save Susan but made a quick, silent plea, *God, take away my fear. I put my trust in thee.* He felt the material, *so lightweight to afford such great protection*, he reasoned.

"Doctor Benz, do your part," Tooms said and stared past Milton.

"Have a seat on the couch," Benz said. Milton turned about, sat on the couch and stared at the white bandages in Benz's hand. Benz read the questioning look and waved the white material as he leaned over Milton. "Bulletproof cloth." He began wrapping the material around Milton's head, covering his head completely from his eyebrows to the top of his head. "I want my future son-in-law protected from any more head trauma."

"You seem to know God's answer," Milton said to Benz.

A Bible appeared before Milton's face. He looked up at the smiling face of Tooms. Milton took the Bible, opened it and gave a chuckle. Empty, but the covers were heavy, he realized. He turned it over, examining it thoroughly. Came the light. He raised his eyes to Tooms. "Bulletproof, no?"

"Yes," Tooms said and sat next to Milton. "Okay, here's the game plan. You..."

"Excuse me Agent Tooms," Benz said and sat in a chair opposite the couch. "Milton, Susan knows that you are not her brother. That seemed to bring her out of melancholy, and give her a noticeable drive to escape this monster. But she's determined there should be no risk to your life to free her."

"Good, Professor," Tooms said and took the Bible from Milton. "When you go up the walk to the house, you will carry this." Tooms stuck Susan's palm pad inside a pocket between the covers of the fake Bible. "That will be connected to my wristwatch from the moment you begin your march up the walk. "Carry it by your side as you take the first steps. This way, cowboy will be satisfied that you are the one approaching the house." Tooms turned Milton's head and puckered up his face. "The guy says he wants you to come to a microphone near the front steps and apologize for ruining his life."

"Have you determined why he suddenly decided to harass me?"

"After his wife moved away she obtained a divorce. He never served time because, according to his probation terms, he went through rehab. We contacted his psychologist after you identified him. She hasn't seen him for months, not since he learned that his ex-wife re-married. She said she could see how he might be upset, but insisted that he has learned to compensate for the fits of rage that got him in trouble before."

Milton glanced at Benz and said, "How do you know Susan is alright? How did you get information to her about her true genetic background?"

"The backup—watch and earplug. We have arranged signals. We talk to her via the earpiece and give her instructions. She lets us know she got our instructions and messages by humming 'Jesus loves me.' Elbergard hasn't caught on yet." Tooms moved the Bible to eye level in front of Milton. "If the van surveillance sees Elbergard raise the rifle when you approach, I will shout through the palm pad, 'Up-up.' You must immediately raise it to eyebrow level and quote a Scripture verse, as if you were reading it from that Bible. That leaves a target on you that is protected by bulletproof cloth—your bandaged head as well. Okay so far?"

Milton nodded, running the plan through his brain. "What about Susan, if Elbergard shoots me? Will she be hurt?"

Tooms glanced at Benz and said, "Foolproof. Before he fires, surveillance will see when he raises the rifle up to the window. If he takes aim, we'll take him out. Our best sharpshooter has the same vision through the curtains, a special scope. He's a hundred yards behind and above the van." Tooms grabbed Milton's hand. "We will do everything possible to avoid shooting, but if he shoots the rifle and sees you are not killed or even if he thinks you are—the impact may knock you on your rear, Milton. Well, if he shoots, we will hit him with a lethal shot before he can harm Susan. Every now and then one has to kill a mad dog. God understands." He made a huge smile for Milton.

Milton recognized his exact words and returned the smile, then felt a frown creep over his face when he verbalized a fear. "You are absolutely certain Susan can't get caught in the crossfire?"

"Absolutely. When Elbergard raises the rifle, Susan knows to lunge forward, exposing Elbergard. Our surveillance confirms that and alerts our sharpshooter. Our guy is the best in the world."

Tooms drove Professor Benz, Guthrie, and Milton to the van. Fetter came out of the van, greeted Milton, and took Benz and Guthrie inside the van. Then yards in front of the van, Tooms stopped Milton. They stood in the middle of the street ninety yards from the white bungalow. Milton scanned his surroundings. The house that held Elbergard and Susan sat between two similarly small clapboard houses, the one closest to the van a dilapidated structure, its gray paint flaking off in many areas. The house to the left of the hostage house sat on the corner and appeared in immaculate shape. How ironic, Milton thought when he noted the flowers lining the walk to the corner house. Next, his eyes rested on the corner street scene. State troopers guarded a rope that restrained a mass of bodies. Milton marveled at the silence of such a large gathering. To his right, movement captured his attention. TV trucks were parked in two of the driveways. Local police appeared to have a struggle containing a small group of photographers and people with cameras and microphones.

"That microphone," Tooms spoke to Milton as they slowly made their way toward the walk of the hostage house, "is just as Elbergard demanded. He wants you to speak into it so the media and the people at the end of the street hear."

The microphone sitting on the walk, halfway between the street and the porch, mocked Milton. He asked Tooms, "What does Elbergard want me to say?"

"He wasn't entirely coherent. The van reviewed the tape several times. We decided he wants an apology from you for causing the breakup of his marriage. He seemed to be saying he wants forgiveness from you, also."

"For what? I should forgive him for stalking me, for kidnapping Susan?"

"Can't be certain, but all of us agreed that he sounded angry, upset and therefore capable of shooting you, the apology and all a ruse to get you in his gun sights."

Perspiration trickled down Milton's back. At first, he attributed it to the bulletproof long underwear. The sun hid behind cloud cover. He surveyed the sky and told himself, *Could be a storm brewing—yeah, and I'm facing i*t. He opened the fake Bible and studied the open palm pad. His mind froze. He wiped sweat off his nose. Looking at Tooms who had stopped at the curb, he asked, "What do I do now?"

The narrow eyebrows and squint told Milton that Tooms was worried. Tooms stepped beside him. "Maybe you shouldn't go through with this. Push the red button. That'll put you in communication with me through my watch-phone and the van will put their surveillance picture on the screen."

"I want to do it. I'm anxious about Susan," he said and pushed the red button. Instantly, the fuzzy outline of figures behind the front-window drapes stared at him. "Neat, Elbergard has Susan positioned between himself and the window. No way to get him."

Faintly, from behind him but louder from the palm pad, he heard Tooms. "Elbergard has Susan tied to him. I told you we have it arranged by signal that Susan will bend down if we need to take him out. Milton, I..."

Milton felt shame at his fear and loss of concentration. "Sorry. I'm okay." He sneaked a quick glance over his shoulder and saw Tooms backpedaling for the van. He stared at the silhouettes on the pad. The one nearest had Susan's Dutch-boy hair and her nose. He imagined the occasional movements were typical for her. The silhouette mostly hidden by Susan could be anyone's, but obviously that of a man, he decided. It seemed like eternity before he reached the microphone.

"You're doing fine. When you get to the microphone, call out Elbergard's name and put the Bible in front of your face and give him your Bible verse," Tooms told him from the palm pad.

One hand clung to the microphone, the other raised the Bible so it covered his head from eyebrows to chin. He struggled to recall the scripture he had decided to relate to Elbergard.

"He has a clean shot at your neck. Lower your chin to your chest like you need to focus on the words, Milton."

The instructions from the pad were crisp, demanding, but he fixed his eyes on the pad screen because the figures shifted somewhat. By lowering the Bible a fraction of an inch he scanned the front window. On each side of the large picture window were two narrow windows. The one toward the door stood wide open. The drapes moved almost imperceptibly, but not for Milton whose senses suddenly became acute. His pulse became rapid. Movement of the opaque curtain hanging over the long window next to the front door caught his attention. He looked at the pad screen and noted two figures remained at the front window. Then he realized the front door stood partially open. The breeze moved the curtain, his mind told him, so he called out, "Joseph Elbergard, this is Milton Heiter." Without waiting he began to recite, "Woe unto the world because of offences! For it must needs be that offences come; but woe to that man by whom the offences cometh!"

Milton moved the Bible down to his chest and immediately heard Tooms screeching through the pad, "Up-up." With a quick jerk Milton brought the Bible directly in front of his face. He shoved his chin onto his chest, but in that instant he noticed the curtain next to the door move. Movement on the screen attracted his full gaze to it. The man silhouette had raised a rifle. It pointed at him. "Jesus, down Jesus," shot out of the palm pad. Susan's silhouette vanished. The man's full silhouette came into focus on the screen.

Milton yelled at the pad, "Tooms, don't shoot. It's..."

"Bang!"

The glass of the large front window exploded. Milton's heart banged against the back of his breastbone. His pulse beat on his eardrums. He swayed, but realized he had not been hit. A white cloth waved out of the partially open front door. Milton heard feet running toward him from the direction of the van. Two bare arms, the hand of one waving a white hankie, protruded through the door first and then a man. Tears had already made their way down to Milton's jaw. He sobbed. He wailed. "Jethroe, not Jethroe."

From beside Milton, Tooms yelled to the figure on the front porch. "Elbergard, keep your hands high and slowly come off the porch."

Men in swat team gear, each with a semiautomatic, dashed for the porch. Two wrestled the disheveled-looking Elbergard to the sidewalk in front of the porch. Three other armed men bolted into the house.

"Susan—Susan," erupted from Milton with the volume of a bullhorn. He started to run for the porch but a vise grip on his arm stopped him. He turned and glared at Tooms. "You killed Jethroe. Three people were in the house. Why? What happened to your fancy high tech?"

He felt warmth on his right. A gentle squeeze from an arm around his waist moved his head to the right. Guthrie cast a tearful smile at him. To her right, Professor Benz, looking ten years older than an hour ago, watched the front door. Anguish froze his face. Milton didn't catch Tooms's excuse for shooting Jethroe, because at that time two swat team men appeared on the front porch. Susan, the left side of her white coat speckled red, trembled in the grasp of the men. Milton searched her figure, analyzed her movements. Susan's head jerked up. When her eyes landed on Milton, she wrenched loose and in four strides fell in his arms.

Between sobs she wailed, "Jethroe, poor Jethroe. Oh, Milton. So horrible. His brains…"

Milton squeezed so hard Susan quit talking. He pulled her coat off and let it hit the ground. "Tell me you aren't hurt."

Susan pushed back and searched his eyes. "Not physically." She looked him up and down, making a curious face at the bandage on his head. "And you? That new bandage…"

Milton began removing the bulletproof wrap on his head and said, "I'm fine. No, I'm crushed. No, I'm thankful you are safe."

Susan leaned over and kissed her father when he put an arm around her shoulders. With the three so close, Milton could see the older Benz's wet cheeks, his bloodshot eyes, the incessant quivering of his lower lip. Guthrie leaned against Milton's back, her arms around his waist. She emitted soft sobs.

"God's second answer, Milton. That was it," Susan said, and stared at him.

"What answer—the message that you are my sister wasn't God's. He doesn't give incorrect answers."

She turned Milton's head toward her. "You strode up that walk ready to die for me, to save my life. God answered. He wants us to marry." Tears streamed down her cheeks. Milton squeezed her hard.

Four swat team men walked by carrying a body bag. Tooms followed until Susan shouted, "Why, Maxwell? Why?"

Haughtily, Tooms surveyed the four tearful people, held together by arms and the glue of unfathomable sadness. "We had no way of knowing that was Jethroe tied to you or that Elbergard gave Jethroe the empty squirrel rifle as a decoy."

"He told you he meant no harm to Milton. He wanted Jethroe as insurance so you wouldn't kill him before he got to talk to Milton."

"Collateral damage, Benz. Not uncommon in terrorist situations," Tooms said and peered over the group.

Milton, followed his gaze. Two men had Elbergard, his hands cuffed behind him, in tow. As they passed the group, Elbergard pulled up, forcing his guards to stop. His eyes burned into Milton's. "Eye for eye, tooth for tooth, Heiter," he scowled. He looked at Susan and added, "Exodus twenty-one. You took away from me two years ago. I took away from you today." He made a sick chuckle and said, "I did not. They did." He turned a mean face to Tooms, "God says, 'Thou shalt not kill.' You are going to hell."

"Part of the job because of scum like you, Elbergard," Tooms said as the guards hauled Elbergard to a waiting patrol car parked alongside the FBI van. Tooms eased over to Milton, sadness written all over his face. "I hate it. But Susan and you are safe. Cowboy..."

Susan wiggled free from Milton's arms and with hands on hips said, "That is not cowboy. Not the one I saw in the clinic or in the hall of my apartment."

Tooms exhaled, his shoulders sagged. He shrugged his shoulders and bolted for the van. Fetter came out of the van and stopped while Tooms talked to him. The group of four started for the van and were met by Fetter. "I'll drive you all to the parsonage," he said. "I have a minivan at the corner." Milton's eyes followed his finger. He marveled at the speed with which the crowd had dispersed. When they were ten yards from the corner, a half dozen people hurried down a drive. Milton noticed the cameras and microphones of the media.

"Excuse me, Reverend Heiter. It's Katherine Hardin from ABC. We talked a couple weeks ago." She stopped three feet in front of him. A cameraman stood at her side. Both blocked his path to Fetter's van.

Milton noted the blonde hair, the pretty, innocent-appearing face. "I remember how you distorted the interview. I experienced your definition of balanced and fair reporting," he said.

"Not us. The local stations did that," Hardin said and thrust a microphone close to his face. "What do you think of your war on stem cell research now? Your young friend was shot. The FBI will call it collateral damage."

The hairs on the back of Milton's neck bristled. "I make war only against those who kill embryos to get stem cells, not those that use stem cells from cord blood or adult tissues."

"Is it worth the price?" Hardin's eyes revealed panic. She waved the microphone at him.

He ignored her question. "With your not-so-hidden agenda you tell your listeners that school prayer, the church's claim that embryos and fetuses are beings is based on old-fashioned extreme radical views that modern Christians don't believe."

When the camera shifted to her, the scowl transformed into a demure smile. "Why Reverend, are you saying we act like the antichrist in our news reporting?"

As Milton pushed by her he said, "No. You are the Antichrist."

Arriving at the parsonage, Milton noticed that cars filled the parking lot. And cars parked along the road in front. An orange glow came from the church windows. All the way from the hostage house the four occupants had remained silent. Only Fetter kept up a running monologue about the wonders of the FBI and the difficulty and bizarre happenings in hostage situations.

Fetter dropped them off in the church parking lot. Professor Benz and Guthrie followed Milton for the front door. Susan walked silently beside Milton until he put his hand on the handle to the church door. She put her hand on top of his. He looked at her.

"I am not your sister, Milton," she said, a coquettish smile moving across her face.

He smiled, letting his eyes speak of love. "I know, Susan. Patience. God is faithful to all who believe. He has spoken. The cost hurts." He opened the door and let Susan enter the sanctuary first. Guthrie and the older Benz followed. Lights were turned off, but a hundred candles made ghoulish features on the heads that turned toward them. Silence fell over the occupants. The exhortative prayer stopped, unfinished, for its leader sat. With Susan at his side, Milton strode to the front, turned, smiled down at Susan and watched Guthrie and Benz find a spot to stand among the shadows of a wall.

"Yea, though I walk through the valley of the shadow of death, I will fear no evil: for thou art with me; thy rod and thy staff they comfort me." The reason for using that scripture to tell the parishioners what was in his heart numbed him. It jabbed his soul.

Tears ran down his cheeks. "Jethroe…" Milton wiped his cheeks with the back of his hand, buying time to find his voice. He put his hand over his eyes and wept convulsively. Throughout the church hankies appeared, audible sobs filled the air. In a low voice he pleaded, "Help me, God. I'm supposed to lead them, help them."

Susan stepped in front of Milton and raised a hand. "When Jethroe and I were tied together," Susan began in a low voice and increased the volume as she spoke. "I prayed for Milton's safety, because I knew Elbergard, a true son of the devil, used Jethroe, the pastor's friend—a friendship that consumed him with Christian love—Elbergard used us as bait. Jethroe, the young man some call unschooled, a hillbilly, prayed." Susan eased to the center of the church and raised the other hand. "Hear his prayer. Jethroe raised his head to the ceiling and said, 'Oh Lord, have mercy on me. Pastor Heiter is my shepherd. I give my life for his. I offer my life to protect this doctor here. I fear not, heavenly father.' Jethroe had no fear in that house of death. Please, find it in your hearts to pray for Joseph Elbergard. Let's not let unforgivingness and hatred infect us in this congregation." Susan lowered her hands and stepped beside Milton.

Subtly, he squeezed her upper arm and stepped forward. "I'm truly humbled by Jethroe's act of love and friendship. Jesus taught his disciples, 'Love each other as I have loved you. Greater love has no one than this, that one lay down his life for his friends.' I will never have a greater friend than Jethroe. He not only laid down his life in order to save mine, but also for the one dearest to me. And what a save Jethroe accomplished." He threw his head toward Susan. "For this medical doctor, this scientist believes that when two DNAs join, a being exists, not at some time that the scientific world proclaims, a claim without fact. How did Doctor Benz find this out? God told her. She listened. And before you stand religion and science united, the old war between them ended by God. But the stem cell wars go on. Jethroe must not have died needlessly. We must continue the battle against Curewell Clinics, the antichrist media, the politically correct, spiritually bankrupt politicians."

"Amen," the congregation said with one loud voice.

"Please stand," Milton said. When the clamor subsided and all faces waited his instructions, he said, "Let us close with 'Amazing Grace.'" Murmurs filled the structure. Milton began to line the song.

"Amazing grace…"

THE END

**Other available books written by Loren Humphrey:**

*Medical Blemishes: Untrue Stories about Real Problems* is a collection of 16 short stories. Allegorical with a surprise ending, each entertains while stimulating the reader's search for truth.

Order from Jenkins LTD for $17.20 ($13.95 plus $3.25 S/H).

*Extreme Cancers* is a novel about hope. A pastor and his younger brother, a cancer surgeon, portray the age-old battle of God versus science as they minister to the cancer patient.

Order from Jenkins LTD for $23.90 ($19.95 plus $3.95 S/H).

*Quinine and Quarantine: Missouri Medicine through the Years*, published by the University of Missouri Press, is the tenth book in the Missouri Heritage Readers Series. This unique book presents medical problems and advances as an integral part of environmental risks and diseases that threatened the citizens of Missouri.

Order from University of Missouri Press, (800) 828-4498 for $9.95.

# *Embryo Factory: The Stem Cell Wars*
# Order Form

**Postal orders:**  Jenkins LTD
503 Nifong #201
Columbia, MO 65201-3717

**Telephone orders:** (573) 874-9243

**E-mail orders:** lorenh@tranquility.net

**Please send** *Embryo Factory: The Stem Cell Wars* **to:**

Name: _____

Address: _____

City: _____  State: _____

Zip: _____

Telephone: (_____) _____

**Book Price: $14.95**

**Shipping:**  $3.00 for the first book and $1.00 for each additional book to
cover shipping and handling within US, Canada, and Mexico.
International orders add $6.00 for the first book and $2.00 for
each additional book.

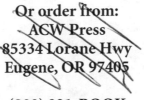

**Or order from:**
**ACW Press**
**85334 Lorane Hwy**
**Eugene, OR 97405**

**(800) 931-BOOK**

or contact your local bookstore